Hide and Seek: Life Lessons of a Geocacher
By
Gary Slinkard

What is geocaching? Geocaching is the outdoor recreational activity, in which participants use a Global Positioning System (GPS) receiver to hide and seek containers at specific locations marked by coordinates all over the world. But it is so much more than that! It is where it takes you to find them, it's the people you meet and the challenge of the hunt. Gary takes you beyond the container and log and opens up the world of adventure around us and the adventure within us that has too often been lost. Journey with him as he gives you the life lessons, the joy and the true treasure waiting to be found!

Book Layout © 2017 BookDesignTemplates.com

Hide and Seek: Life Lessons of a Geocacher / Gary Slinkard. -- 1st ed.

ISBN: 978-1541026537

Dedication

This book is dedicated to:

My wonderful wife Susan, who is the "wind beneath my wings". She is the greatest wife, mother, and woman that I have ever met and on top of all that, she is far superior at geocaching than I am. You are the world to me and I love you dearly.

To my boys: Caleb, Josh, and Nathan who have been such a blessing in my life that it would take 1,000 books to describe what you mean to me. I love you guys so much and am very proud of the men that you have become!

Quotations

"Even the good plans of wise wizards like Gandalf and of good friends like Elrond go astray sometimes when you are off on dangerous adventures over the Edge of the Wild, and Gandalf was a wise enough wizard to know it."
— J.R.R. Tolkien

"It's a dangerous business, Frodo, going out your door. You step onto the road, and if you don't keep your feet, there's no knowing where you might be swept off to."
— J.R.R. Tolkien, The Lord of the Rings

"Not all those who wander are lost."
— J.R.R. Tolkien, The Fellowship of the Ring

Or as we say today, not all who wander are lost...some are GEOCACHING!

CONTENTS

CHAPTER ONE

THE SPORT OF GEOCACHING

Is geocaching a sport? I like to refer to it as a sport but if you prefer you can call it a hobby, game, obsession, or any other label that you feel comfortable giving it. Why do I call it a sport? I have my reasons.

The term sport has become a fun discussion point between me and my lovely wife, Susan. For example, she has always called figure skating a sport and me always, jokingly, called it a competition since it required judges to decide who won or lost instead of who was the fastest or who scored the most points, etc.

I have changed my stance some over the years as I have gotten older and while figure skating has now started to include a certain amount of measurable aspects, I can see it as a sport now as well as geocaching. Here's the definition of "sport" in case you are wondering:

"an athletic activity requiring skill or physical prowess and often of a competitive nature"[1]

Though I am not a competitive geocacher, there are those that fit into this category which we will discuss later. Geocaching does fit into the athletic activity part most of the time. It does require skill see the chapter on "geosenses". Physical prowess can play a role and a healthy one at that (see more in the chapter on Health). So, overall, I think I have defended my definition of calling it a sport.

There's something about the adventure and the life lessons associated with geocaching that I have very strong feelings about and that led me to write this book. I've tried in the past to explain to someone why geocaching has affected me so much and why it is something you shouldn't overlook. I think I have never been able to articulate it as well as I would have liked before I decided to write this book. I hope I have laid out for you a compelling case in the pages ahead. Let's begin with a formal definition of geocaching:

"Geocaching /ˈdʒiːoʊˌkæʃɪŋ/ is an outdoor recreational activity, in which participants use a Global Positioning System (GPS) receiver or mobile device and other navigational techniques to hide and seek containers, called "geocaches" or "caches", at specific locations marked by coordinates all over the world."[2]

That is the formal definition and it is helpful but it is also good to have a "working" definition. A definition that can be your "go to" definition when you are asked what geocaching is and trust me if you continue in the sport going forward you are going to be asked what it is many times.

I like the definition I came up with a few years ago:

"it's treasure hunting where the treasure is the hunt!"

Not bad, huh? I think it captures part of the greatness and adventure that awaits you. Sure, there is SWAG – Stuff We All Get and there are trackables to move along on their mission and the logbook which you must sign to prove you were there but we will get to those later. The things that make geocaching so great are the life lessons and the adventure!

Let's also get a working definition of adventure:

1. an undertaking usually involving danger and unknown risks
2. the encountering of risks <the spirit of adventure>
3. an exciting or remarkable experience[3]

That's a pretty good way to capture what adventure means and it is so true to geocaching.

We will talk about danger and risks in this book and how to deal with them but also, I will capture the excitement of this remarkable experience!

Discovery is not just the piece of Tupperware® or the glorious Bison Tube[4] or the nano...ah yes, the wonderful nano and yes, I love those little guys. Every geocache has a place but only in the correct space. Nice rhyme, Gary.

The discovery is the places you go and let me tell you there are places you didn't know existed until geocaching leads you to them. Places not labeled on maps, places down an unmarked dirt road, or a cool hidden lake, a back forest trail or up the side of a lonely mountain. It could just be a part of town you have never ventured into or a road you have never driven down. Those places are out there and they have geocaches, around 3 million of them and that number is growing all the time!

When I was very young I read a Reader's Digest article about a treasure that was on Oak Island (covered in Chapter 2). The History Channel began airing the series on January 5, 2014, about that place called, "The Curse of Oak Island". I loved the article as a kid and I love the show now in its fourth season at the writing of this book.

Also, when I was young, a movie came out that I really loved. The name of that movie was Raiders of the Lost Ark. I was fascinated by the adventure of the hunt in that movie. I guess the idea of searching for something that was lost or hidden for a long time has a thrill to it that is very hard for some to understand.

Something that I'm NOT going to do in this book is to give you what I call "home movies". The detailed exploits of me finding a geocache may have been an adventure to me but you reading about it isn't that exciting. Those types of stories really do fall into the "you had to be there" category.

It's true that some people like to watch other people's home movies but those are rare souls. I guess in many ways Facebook and to some extent, Twitter is very much like that so that is something that I'm not going to do here (well, very rarely, but only to drive home a point).

What I AM going to do is capture the thrill, the adventure, the excitement and the life lessons and in the end hopefully the reasons why you should become a geocacher as well. I hope that my persuasion has at least gotten you to read a little bit more of this book! Keep reading! We are about to discuss the adventure of a lifetime!!

CHAPTER TWO

WHERE ADVENTURE BEGAN

The Four-Leaf Clover

When I was very young, I remember watching my dad look down on the ground when we were outside or we were waiting for others to go out to eat or something and I finally asked him one day what he was doing. He told me he was looking at the clover trying to find one with four leaves.

From time to time, he would find one and show me. I was never very good at finding them but it was something I enjoyed doing with my dad so even if I couldn't find one it was still a good moment or two of adventure with him.

In case you aren't familiar with the significance, four-leaf clovers are a symbol of good luck so people have looked for them for centuries. They are pretty rare on the order of 10,000 to 1 but not impossible to find.[5]

My dad passed away in 2001. I think he would have loved geocaching. He certainly had the heart of a geocacher.

The Oak Island Mystery

As I mentioned in Chapter 1, when I was a kid, I read this Reader's Digest article[6]

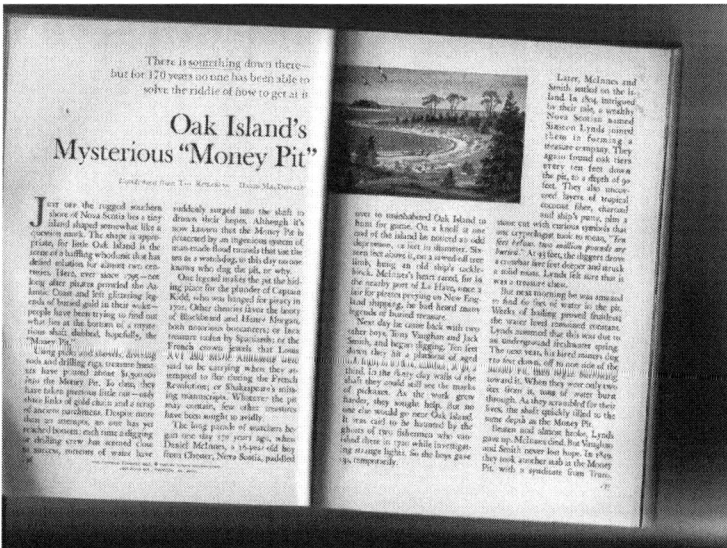

This was a big boost to my adventurous nature. As a kid, finding buried treasure was a dream too good to be true! Needless to say, I buried my share of trinkets and "treasure" just like I had read about many times before in books and magazines. Hmm, I wonder if I ever dug all my treasures back up? I guess someone next century might find one of my plastic army men that I left behind and claim it as a rare treasure!

"For more than a century and a half, there have been investigations and excavations on Oak Island. There are a large number of theories about what might be buried or concealed on the Island. Areas of interest on the island include a location known as the Money Pit, a formation of boulders called "Nolan's Cross", the beach at "Smith's Cove", and a triangle-shaped "Swamp".[7] The Money pit area has been repeatedly excavated. Critics argue that there is no treasure and that the Money Pit is a natural phenomenon."[8]

Here is an excerpt from Wikipedia on the Oak Island Mystery

Money Pit at Oak Island

There are many 19th-century accounts of Oak Island, but some are conflicting or biased.[9] Further, physical evidence from the initial excavations is unavailable. A basic summary of the history of the pit is as follows:

In 1857, there appeared newspaper accounts of a group digging for the treasure of the pirate Captain Kidd on Oak Island.[10] In 1862, treasure hunter J.B. McCully of Truro, Nova Scotia wrote that the early settlers of the Oak Island area had brought with them a story of a dying sailor of Captain Kidd's crew claiming that 2 million pounds' value in treasure had been buried on an island. McCully further claimed that in the early days of settlement, a "Mr. McGinnis" while scouting a location for a farm had happened upon a depression in the earth which was consistent with the "Captain Kidd" story. With the assistance of a "Smith" and "Vaughn", McCully claimed that McGinnis excavated the depression and discovered a layer of flagstones two feet below. As they dug down they discovered layers of logs at about every 10 feet (3.0 m). They were said to have abandoned the excavation at 30 feet (9.1 m) due to the people of the area refusing to assist in the digging based on "superstitious dread".[11] In 1863, an investor in the Oak Island diggings named Paul Phy claimed that "McGinnis" was the first settler on Oak Island and had discovered the "depression" around 1799.[12]

Investigator Joe Nickell reviewed the original accounts and interviews with McGinnis descendants and other descendants of the original Oak Island land owners. While later sources asserted that the treasure had been discovered by three young boys, he asserted that the story was of three adult lot owners who discovered the depression on the island and began digging.[13]

These excavations were first briefly mentioned in print in the Liverpool Transcript in October 1856. A complete account followed, again in the Liverpool Transcript, by a Justice of the Peace in Chester, Nova Scotia,[14] the Novascotian,[15] British Colonist,[16] and A History of Lunenburg County[17] (the last source based on the Liverpool Transcript articles).

At the writing of this book, the next season of the "Curse of Oak Island" began on November 15, 2016.[18] So far, they haven't found anything of monetary value other than some British coins from the 1700's and one old Spanish copper 8 maravedis (how did THAT get there?) but the "Fellowship of the Dig" as they call themselves has said that even though their main goal is finding the treasure, they have enjoyed the process and the friendships they have made during this process. Sometimes, that is as valuable as gold.

Their adventure continues and the treasure may be all but gone from the island but they inspire people to this day to not give up and to not abandon the search for treasure in any form.

King Tut and the Egyptian Tombs

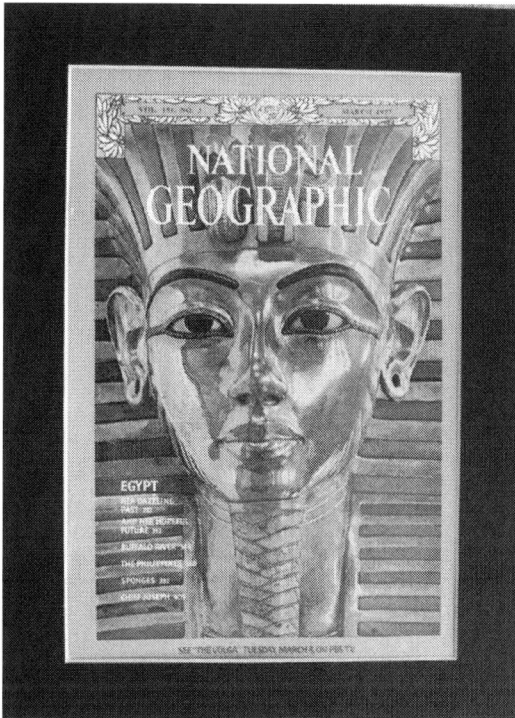

Another closely viewed treasure find for me, came from the pages of a March 1977 National Geographic and the incredible story of the tomb of King Tutankhamun. This wasn't like Oak Island, they were showing us the actual located TREASURE!

It had been found and there were the pictures of this great discovery right there in the magazine and it was all that a boy wrapped up in the spirit of adventure could handle! Seeing it, as a kid on those colorful and well-documented pages of the magazine were breathtaking and still are even to this day.

Howard Carter's discovery captured the world and most certainly captured this kid's imagination. "On 4 November 1922, Howard Carter's excavation group found steps that Carter hoped led to Tutankhamun's tomb (subsequently designated KV62) (the tomb that would be considered the best preserved and most intact pharaonic tomb ever found in the Valley of the Kings).

He wired Lord Carnarvon to come, and on 26 November 1922, with Carnarvon, Carnarvon's daughter and others in attendance, Carter made the "tiny breach in the top left-hand corner" of the doorway (with a chisel his grandmother had given him for his 17th birthday.) He was able to peer in by the light of a candle and see that many of the gold and ebony treasures were still in place. He did not yet know whether it was "a tomb or merely a **cache**", but he did see a promising sealed doorway between two sentinel statues. When Carnarvon asked "Can you see anything?", Carter replied with the famous words:

"Yes, wonderful things!"[19]

Did you notice that? Did you see what Howard called it? A CACHE! Yes, my friends, that was an early form of geocaching... just without the "geo" part!

Many years later, I was able to recapture some of that childhood excitement at an encore of the exhibition in the United States which ran at the Dallas Museum of Art from October 2008 to May 2009.[20]

I'm sure that Susan and the boys enjoyed the exhibit and it was massive! It was laid out in several rooms and I just remember that it was very hard dragging me out of that place that day.

Raiders of the Lost Ark

Just a scant four years later in 1981, my adventurous heart got another jolt when this came to my local theater, "Raiders of the Lost Ark". From the retrieving of the golden idol in Peru to the recovery of the headstone of the staff of Ra, the movie was one amazing adventure after another that lead up to the final discovery of the Ark of the Covenant and the finale was just amazing movie-making.

Here was a cool adventurer, treasure hunter, bad-ass that dared to find those precious artifacts that as he would say, "belong in a museum"! He never backed down from a fight and he knew when to bring a gun to a sword fight!

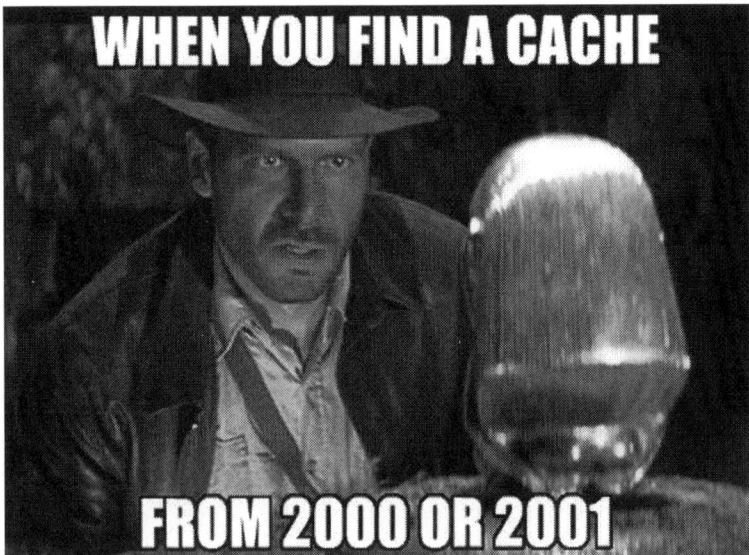

WHEN YOU FIND A CACHE FROM 2000 OR 2001

Apparently, I am not the only one that ties Indiana Jones to geocaching. You can see now

why adventure is in the blood of geocachers and is
in my blood too! It has always been there.

The Hobbit/ The Lord of the Rings

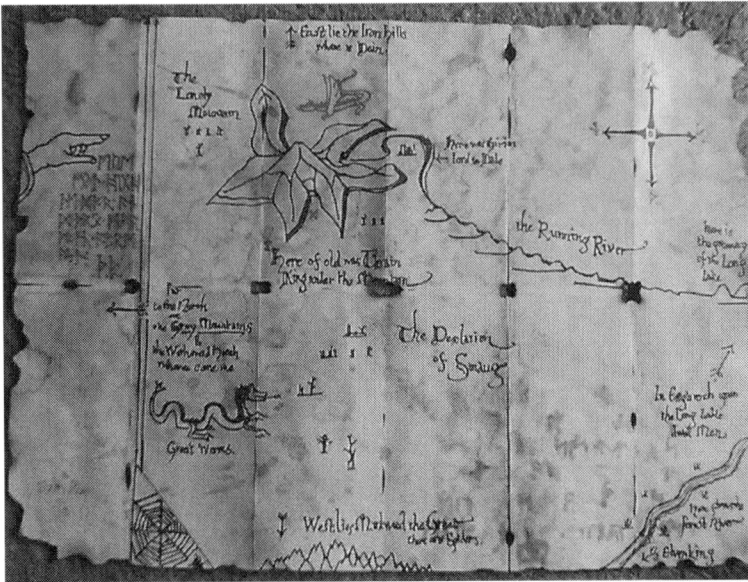

I first read "The Hobbit" in 1982 in my senior year High School literature class. Oops, I gave away my age. Yes, I am old but let's forget about that and get back to the story. I did quote from these great works back at the beginning of the book. Did you skip over it? Mark this spot, go back and read them. Are you back now? OK, let's continue.

I read the Hobbit and all three of the Lord of the Rings books out loud to Susan and the kids before each "Lord of the Rings" movie came out back in 2001-2003 and I highly recommend reading these books with your friends or family. They are some of the greatest adventure books ever written.

One note that I want to make here is an item in the book that really caught my attention back when I first read it and that was the Moon Runes:

In Chapter 3 of "The Hobbit", as the company stays in Rivendell, Elrond is able to discover that the map contained moon letters which were rune letters that were only visible on the evening when there was a moon of the same shape and in the same season as the evening they were written.

The runes on the map, therefore, were written on a midsummer's eve when a crescent moon shone behind them. They were written in silver pen using ithildin which was a derivative of Mithril and was used by the dwarves to decorate gateways, pathways, and portals. The moon letters on Thror's map are written as follows:

ᚢᛏᚠᛤ·ᛒᛰ·ᚦᛖ·ᚷᚱᛖᛰ·ᚢᛏᛖᛁᛖ·ᚻᚹᛖᛘᛏᚦᛖ
·ᚦᚱᚢᚢᚻ·ᚻᛁᚠᚲᚻᚢ·ᚠᛏᚾ·ᚦᛖ·ᚢᛖᛏᛏᛜ·ᚢᚿ
ᛏ·ᛈᛁᚦ·ᚦᛖ·ᛚᚠᚢᛏ·ᛚᛁᚷᚻᛏ·ᚠᚹ·ᛤᚢᚱᚻᚢ·ᛘᚠ
ᛤ·ᛈᛁᛚᛚ·ᚢᚻᚻᛖ·ᚢᚲᛖᛏ·ᚦᛖ·ᚻᛖᛘᚠᚻᛏᛖ·
·ᚦ·

"Stand by the grey stone when the thrush knocks, and the setting sun with the last light will shine on Durin's Day will shine upon the key-hole" Written by Thrain.[21]

Here again is that unique aspect to the adventure Bilbo and the Dwarves had to deal with and even though they were reluctant to get help from the elves they broke down and accepted their help. Very much like me and puzzle caches! I promise I will get better at them! One of my Christmas presents this year was, "How to Puzzle Cache" by Cully Long.

National Treasure

Another movie that reminds me of geocaching and fueled my adventurous spirit even further was "National Treasure". The movie came out in 2004, two years before I started geocaching. It's sequel which was really good for most movie sequels was "National Treasure: The Book of Secrets" which came out three years later in 2007. We are still waiting for them to do National Treasure 3 but it might happen so keep an eye out for it.

Cage plays Benjamin Franklin Gates, a historian and amateur cryptologist searching for a lost treasure of precious metals, jewelry, artwork and other artifacts that was accumulated into a single massive stockpile by looters and warriors over many millennia starting in Ancient Egypt, later rediscovered by warriors who form themselves into the Knights Templar to protect the treasure, eventually hidden by American Freemasons during the American Revolutionary War.

A coded map on the back of the Declaration of Independence points to the location of the "national treasure", but Gates is not alone in his quest. Whoever can steal the Declaration and decode it first will find the greatest treasure in history.[22]

The need for the characters to search for clues in so many different locations reminds me of a really good multi-cache! From the search for the Meerschaum pipe in the ship up at the Arctic Circle that was used at the end of the movie to open the secret treasure door, to the Ottendorf cipher that is discovered on the back of the U. S. Declaration of Independence, to using the "Silence Dogood" letters as the key text really created a great movie adventure.

Using lemon juice and heat to reveal invisible writing and then on top of that to have that writing be the cipher just blew me away! Even down to one of the clues being, "Heere at the Wall" as an homage to the original name for Broadway, DeHeere Street, and the Wall means Wall Street, which follows the path of a wall the Dutch built that leads them to the next clue.

Another aspect of geocaching in the movie was the location of the special Ben Franklin spectacles hidden beneath a brick at Independence Hall. The fact that you could not find the correct brick without the steeple pointing to it by the use of a shadow. The fact that they used archeoastronomy[23], which I am also fascinated with and a topic for another book, was just incredible!

Also, that the clue was hidden in a $100 bill was just another awesome detail. What's incredible is that many geocaches around the world use these kinds of details, clues, and hints and they are just waiting for you to find them. Now that's adventure!

CHAPTER THREE

BEGINNINGS IN GEOCACHING

The year was 2000 and the U.S. government had removed the "selective availability" they had placed on GPS technology thus making a GPS receiver ten times more accurate than ever before.

For GPS enthusiasts, this was definitely a cause for celebration. Internet newsgroups suddenly teemed with ideas about how the technology could be used.

One such enthusiast, Dave Ulmer, a computer consultant, wanted to test the accuracy by hiding a navigational target in the woods. He called the idea the "Great American GPS Stash Hunt" and posted it in an internet GPS users' group. The idea was simple: Hide a container out in the woods and note the coordinates with a GPS unit.

The finder would then have to locate the container with only the use of his or her GPS receiver. The rules for the finder were simple: "Take some stuff, leave some stuff."

On May 3rd, he placed his own container, a black bucket, in the woods near Beavercreek, Oregon, near Portland. Along with a logbook and pencil, he left various prize items including videos, books, software, and a slingshot. He shared the waypoint of his "stash" with the online community on sci.geo.satellite-nav:

N 45° 17.460 W 122° 24.800

Within three days, two different readers read about his stash on the Internet, used their own GPS receivers to find the container, and shared their experiences online. Throughout the next week, others excited by the prospect of hiding and finding stashes began hiding their own containers and posting coordinates. Like many new and innovative ideas on the Internet, the concept spread quickly - but this one required leaving your computer to participate.

Within the first month, Mike Teague, the first person to find Ulmer's stash, began gathering the online posts of coordinates around the world and documenting them on his personal home page. The "GPS Stash Hunt" mailing list was created to discuss the emerging activity. Names were even tossed about to replace the name "stash" due to the negative connotations of that name. One such name was "geocaching."[24]

A typical cache is a small waterproof container containing a logbook (with a pen or pencil). The geocacher enters the date they found it and signs it with their established code name. After signing the log, the cache must be placed back exactly where the person found it.

Larger containers such as plastic storage containers (Tupperware or similar) or ammunition boxes can also contain items for trading, such as toys or trinkets, usually of more sentimental worth than financial.

Geocaching shares many aspects with benchmarking, trigpointing, orienteering, treasure-hunting, letterboxing, and waymarking.[25]

Susan and I started Geocaching in 2006. It started with my interests in GPS and subsequently purchasing a GPSr, a Magellan Meridian Gold (pictured below). I remember one day we were going out to lunch at work and I was looking at the GPSr and, by the way, I was not driving. We are going down the street in town and I told the guys in the car, "hey, we are about to go over a creek!" And we did just then. Okay, I was impressed! The guys in the car were as well. I guess I'm not the only one!

Nowadays, pretty much everyone in the civilized world uses this technology and, for the most part, takes it for granted. To this day, I don't. I am still fascinated by the process. Maybe it's being observant or more in tune with my surroundings so that even turning on a light switch to me is still magic.

So here I was with a GPSr and noticing where a creek was had become my one and only trick and, as Susan said, I needed to come up with another reason why I spent money on this gadget. So, I started searching the Internet for more information and ran across geocaching. Now, this was back when there were no smartphones or at least I didn't have one and we were just learning how this device even worked.

We would print out a handful of geocaches for the day's hunt and hoped that we could find one or two. Susan would carefully mark each page whether we found it or didn't find it and that night I would log them in on the Geocaching.com website. We are still not the fastest geocachers out there that but we have had a few days where we have found 24 geocaches in 24 hours. This is probably just a morning hunt for some but we tend to not move that fast.

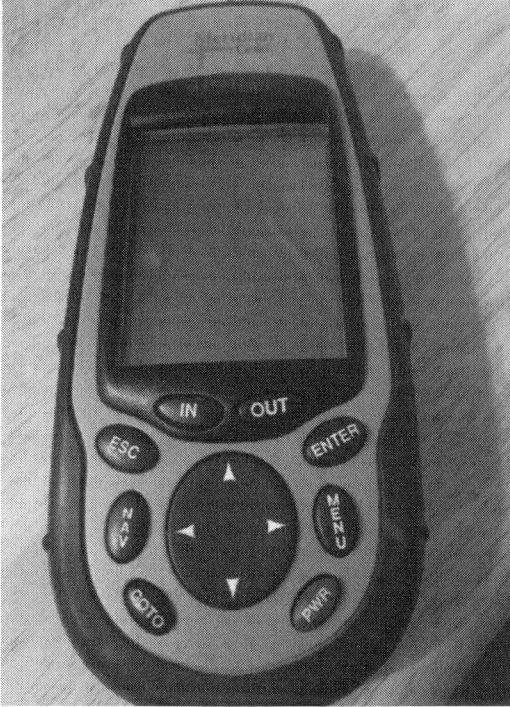

Still, in today's higher tech world, we move at a much faster pace than we use to geocache. Nowadays, we mostly use our smartphones. I know for many that is sacrilege! One thing to make note of is that for us and where we live lends itself to using a smartphone.

Now if we lived in an area without reliable cell service, then I would see a greater need to use my GPSr more often. While traveling, this is something that we are aware of and for yourself, this is something that you need to not forget to plan.

Whatever tool that you use, make sure that you are comfortable using it and that the technology doesn't hinder your fun of geocaching. Remember, the point is that you enjoy it not that you are doing the sport the way that someone else does the sport. After all, if you are not enjoying it then what is the point?

We hid our first cache, GCXY9M, "Happy Hunt-ing" (I live in Hunt County and yes, it's cheesy) on 8/24/2006. It ended up being found 114 times and was a drum roll please, a camouflaged pill bottle. Ok, it wasn't the greatest geocache of all time but cachers enjoyed it and it brought some joy to them. We actually hid three that day and one of them, Warren Peace, GCXY9R, is still alive. If you ever need 8/2006 on your Jasmer grid it's still alive over 10 years later and I would be honored if you came and found it. I'll keep it alive for you until then.

Susan and I have gone on to hide over 100 geocaches and found over 1,000 and we are not done yet. We have had our activity hampered by "life" from time to time but I don't see us ever stopping!

CHAPTER FOUR

OBSTACLES

In a great sport like geocaching, there will be obstacles. Helen Keller said, "the marvelous richness of human experience would lose something of rewarding joy if there were no limitations to overcome. The hilltop hour would not be half so wonderful if there were no dark valleys to traverse."[26] Now, this doesn't compare to what Helen Keller overcame but I like the quote and it seemed to be a good way to describe overcoming obstacles to reach a joyous and grand thing in your life.

So, with that understanding, I bring you a series of obstacles inspired by my friend, Keith Petrus, and his FTF Magazine path tags series known as "Geo-Nemesis". This is by no means is an exhaustive list but should get you started on thinking about what your obstacles may be for you.

Geo-Nemesis #1 – Wasps, Hornets or Bees

One day, Susan and I were out at a cemetery cache. Here in Texas, many of the best hiding spots are either in parks or cemeteries. It seems that there are a lot of places that would be good to hide a geocache but often it is on private property or so often we are told. I am not sure how it happened that the friendly state (that's what Texas means Tejas) became such an unfriendly location for geocaching but everywhere you go, there is a fence.

We searched for a while and then I spotted the cache. Now as I have mentioned before, Susan is a much better geocacher than I am but this time, I was the one that saw it.

It was a camouflaged pill bottle at the end of a chain-link fence where the fence had come loose. The container fits perfectly at the end of that loosened fence piece.

After grabbing the cache, I handed it to Susan because she writes much better than I do and if that log is going to be legible, she needs to be the one to sign it. After she signed the log, I started to put the geocache back and there they were! Lots of yellow hornets! I must've disturbed them when I pulled the geocache out of the fence.

So now what do I do? As a good geocacher, you need to put the container back where you found it, right? The geocacher's creed is to not try and "fix" the geocache location with what you think might be a better one. It needed to go back exactly as I had found it but in this case, that rule posed a problem. What to do! Ah, below the fence, there was a location where you could put flowers. So, my solution was to place it there as close as possible to where the cache was originally located and then contact the cache owner and let them know what I had to do.

Geo-Nemesis #2 - Ants

Depending on what part of the world you live in, this nemesis can be very painful! Susan and I have sort of a running joke that somehow, they always find her! I guess for her it's not really a joke because it's always painful because around here the type of ants we have are fire ants.

Fire ants after they bite you feel like they're continuing to bite you. For humans, this is a painful sting, a sensation similar to what one feels when burned by fire (hence the name) and the after effects of the sting can be deadly to sensitive people.[27]

It's a good idea to check once in a while where you are standing when you live down here in the southern part of the United States. Just to make sure that they are not beginning their preparation for an attack on your ankle.

Geo-Nemesis #3 – Snakes

This one, of course, depends on the variety that you encounter. Some are poisonous and deadly and others are harmless. For me personally, I just avoid all of them! We have been fortunate to have only seen a couple of snakes over the 10 years that we have been geocaching.

There was one time when I went to retrieve a geocache that I had archived and luckily, I looked down and noticed that the container was covered up by a snake. That will wake you up! Needless to say, that I had to return on another occasion.

There was also one other time when we were able to retrieve a geocache but very close to it was a very small snake that we were able to avoid. I have heard stories of some who have not been as fortunate.

It is important to be aware of your surroundings. There are probably only a few locations in the world where this threat is not present so keep your eyes open at all times while geocaching.

Here are our snake safety tips to remember:

1. Wear the correct clothing! Long sleeves and pants with thick boots that cover the ankle will protect you in the event of a bite.
2. Snakes can strike at a distance of roughly half their length. Keep your distance if you do encounter one, and back away slowly.
3. Never risk it! If you see a snake, consider it to be venomous and treat it as such. Most snake bites come not from someone being surprised, but from people that try to move or even play with snakes.
4. Be careful where you step! A snake can look like a stick or might be lying in the sun trying to stay warm. You need to stay alerted and watch every step you take when in snake country to avoid surprising a snake.
5. Be careful where you put your hands! A longtime friend of mine told me that most snakebites on golf courses come from players, who like myself, spend more time in the rough than on the fairway. They see their ball and reach down to grab it not

realizing that right next the ball was a snake. The same holds true for us as geocachers. Don't let the triumph of finally finding that hidden cache overrides your common sense or alertness to dangers.

6. If you are walking your dog while geocaching in an area where there might be snakes, keep them on a leash to avoid a chance encounter.[28]

Geo-Nemesis #4 – Ticks

Ah, the dreaded tick. Now this one has become such an issue in parts of the world that there are even special ways to remove these pests including a tool of the trade known as a tick key since they can be difficult to remove. Ticks can carry disease so please check thoroughly after a day of geocaching to make sure you haven't brought any home with you.

Here are some additional tips:
1. Know the environment – ticks prefer long grass and moist humid areas. If there is a well-defined trail, stay near the center
2. Common bug sprays work well as a tick repellent
3. Wear light-colored clothing so you can see the tick and remove it
4. Tuck your pants into your socks to prevent ticks from biting your ankles or climbing to your nether regions.
5. When you get home, shower, you and your family will appreciate it
6. Wash your clothes as they can become attached to the clothing and hit you up for a meal later on.
7. Inspect yourself and your pets, common areas are under the arms, around the ears, behind the knees, waist and even inside the belly button
8. Have your pets on a monthly treatment: I use Frontline on my geo-pup[29]

Geo-Nemesis #5 – Spiders

On a recent Geocache Talk podcast[30], my guest on the show was Craig Michell who told us about the spiders down in Australia including the white-tail spider that bit him and caused a series of welts which required an antibiotic to be administered. For Craig, the infection reappears each year which requires further doses of medicine.

Whatever type of spider you have in your area, know what they are and where they tend to hang out before going out geocaching and by all means, do what Craig suggests and poke the possible geocache location with a stick before putting your hand in there!

Geo-Nemesis #6 – Chiggers

I had to mention this one because it is a huge problem where I live and is relatively unknown in other parts of the world so I get asked about them from time to time.

The chigger doesn't actually bite you, it injects a digestive enzyme into the skin that break down skin cells thus causing great irritation, redness, and I hate them with all my being! A true obstacle that I strive to avoid every year!

Chiggers, which are also called harvest mites or red bugs, are very small and cannot usually be seen without a magnifying glass or microscope.

They are a type of parasitic mite, like scabies, but are unlike non-parasitic dust mites that can trigger allergy symptoms.

Surprisingly, you also won't feel it when they "bite" you, which is why you usually don't even know you were around chiggers until you start itching and notice the rash about 12 or 24 hours later.[31]

Geo-Nemesis #7 – Mosquitos and Horse Flies

These creatures pierce the skin and feed on your blood, the little vampires, and in the case of the mosquito, their saliva left after causes great irritation. The horse fly uses its mouth to stab in a slicing motion to cause a cut to draw blood as well. There are other biting insects but you get the idea of these pests. These are obstacles to be ready and prepared for before heading out for a day of geocaching!

So, what is the best method to prevent getting bit? Use DEET! DEET has a bad reputation. But peruse the medical literature, and you'll find adverse reactions to it are rare—and tend to occur only when people swallow or snort the stuff. Like anything you rub on your skin, DEET can cause an allergic reaction in some people. But used as directed, it's basically harmless and extremely effective, Day says. But he's quick to add, most people don't understand how to apply it properly.

First of all, you should NOT spray DEET on your body and clothes like it's perfume, he stresses. Instead, squirt a little onto your hands and rub it onto your ankles, elbows, wrists, forehead, and all the other places where your skin is thin—and where mosquitos love to feed."[32]

Geo-Nemesis #8 – Traffic

You didn't think ALL of the obstacles are of the animal or insect variety, did you? Now, this Geo-Nemesis may seem like a very unusual one. But it is one that you have to maintain an awareness of why you're out geocaching unless you are out in the glorious wilderness. Susan and I have passed by some geocaches because we felt that there wasn't an adequate location to park. Better to be safe than injured or dead!

Now, this doesn't rule out the possibility of planning ahead and doing some investigative work prior to getting to a cache that does not have an adequate location to park. Use the tools that are available to you like Google Earth or some other program, to get you properly navigated.

Many times, you will be able to park across the street or down the street and then just walk up carefully to where the cache is located. Sometimes, you might be able to park a street over or you might be able to park in a designated public parking spot.

I have had some geocachers tell me that what they do is pull up near the cache and put their hazards on but I'm not a fan of this method but at the very least your warning traffic that your car is parked there. Stay safe out there!

CHAPTER FIVE

DISAPPOINTMENTS

In life, as in any sport, there will be disappointments. Some friends of ours who go by the geocaching handle "Memfis Mafia" said that the first geocache they looked for they couldn't find. Now, for some people, they would have just given up but instead, they found the challenge to be rewarding even in the midst of disappointment and so they kept on going and now they have found many geocaches.

The greatest disappointment in geocaching is a "did not find" which you will see as an acronym "DNF" for short. A "did not find" should be logged on the Geocaching.com website whenever you look for a geocache and do not find it. Now, Susan and I have had situations where we were not able to look for the cache and either we ran out of time or there was something blocking our way to get near the cache in those situations we simply logged nothing.

Many geocachers choose not to log anything even if they have looked for the geocache. Of course, the main reason to log a DNF is to let the geocache owner know two things. The first, is that there is a possibility that the geocache is missing. The second is to let fellow geocachers know that someone has looked previously and though they may have just missed it at least there was an attempt.

At this point you have to make a decision, do you skip over the geocache assuming that it truly is missing or do you decide to look for it with at least some knowledge that you may also end up disappointed?

So how should you handle a DNF? Hopefully, you handle it like "Memfis Mafia" did! Our friends tried to find their first cache and didn't find it but they did not give up! They pressed on to other caches, made note of the ones they did not find, and once they found some they went back and avenged those DNF's.

Early on in the sport when you are still a "rookie", you need to realize that geocache hides aren't as easy as you think they are and that you need to "get your legs under you" before you decide that the cache is truly missing.

As a geocacher, avenging a DNF is very sweet! Susan, I had a DNF on our first weekend of geocaching. I marked that geocache and as I like to call them our "white whales" like Ahab called his nemesis whale in the book, Moby Dick. Quite a bit of time had passed before we were able to go back to that area and we found that first DNF geocache after all.

You see, there are many similarities in the sport of geocaching and in life. Sometimes things just don't go as planned but how you react to that uncertainty, disappointment, and unplanned events that occur says a lot about you and your character.

If you are a parent, how you react to these types of situations can be teaching moments for your children or if you react poorly they can be negative teaching moments. Use those types of situations to your advantage.

One thing that I do even to this day is to not claim that the geocache is not there. That is a presumption that many times is incorrect. Instead, what I like to do is say something to the effect that, "today just wasn't our day or we just didn't have any luck". By stating the DNF in this manner, you are accurately stating that indeed you did not find it but that sometimes you just do not have the skills yet, the right angle when you were looking that day, or it was just hidden in a way that you are unfamiliar with to find the cache. There is no shame in a statement like that and it avoids arrogance and many times is the truth.

Another disappointment you may run into while out geocaching is the destroyed or damaged geocache. As a cache owner, these are very disheartening. On many of the geocaches I have created, I have spent hours or sometimes even days creating a quality geocache. When I find that it has been damaged or destroyed by someone whom we typically refer to as a "muggle" (see Glossary of Terms).

Some geocachers at this point decide to do what is called a "throw-down" or an on the spot replacement of the geocache. This is a bad idea because you most certainly do not have all the information on what this geocache requires and even if you contact the owner you are still not able to replace the geocache per Geocaching.com rules.

I can respect this under almost every circumstance but maybe the log is so wet or destroyed that it just needs a fresh one or the container is missing an O-ring and it is causing it to leak. If I can fix the container and save the cache owner a trip out to do exactly what they would do, then I feel that is acceptable. You have to decide yourself what you will do in these situations. If I do not have the adequate supplies with me to fix the geocache, then I let the geocache owner know the status of their geocache and then I move on.

This does bring up another point about geocaching and that is, "is it okay to cheat at geocaching?" Since there really are no hard and fast rules that are enforced by Geocaching.com about logging a find, you could log a find on many caches that you actually do not find but where is the adventure in that?

One of the things that geocachers have to get used to is the possibility of disappointment either as a cache owner or as a geocacher searching for a geocache. I have read many geocache logs from people who were new to the sport who are very surprised when a geocache is either not there (or they think it's not there) or it has been destroyed or damaged.

These types of issues are inevitable. As we all know, if you leave something outside many things are possible. It can become damaged by weather or as in the case of one of my own geocaches it was run over by a lawnmower. Now that geocache was really damaged! I was able to salvage a few pieces. Geocaches have been known to be chewed by an animal, just flat out taken by a squirrel or something, or just eroded over time by heat, rain or some other environmental factor.

Unfortunately, the other major factor resulting in geocaches either going missing or damaged are muggles. For some reason that I really haven't been able to put my finger on, people like to destroy property that is not theirs. As a cache owner, walking up to your own geocache and finding it in pieces is a tough thing to do especially if it is a geocache that you have worked hard to create.

I remember one time I went to check on a birdhouse geocache in sort of a WVTim fashioned gadget cache. I got to Ground Zero and as I looked around my first assumption was that it had been removed. Now, I had secured permission to place this cache in a local park by our local parks department. So, I figured it wasn't removed by one of them but assumed that it was probably a muggle.

As I examine the area closer I did finally spot some pieces and chunks of what was left of the birdhouse. Someone had gone to a lot of trouble to destroy it. I'm assuming that they thought that there was something valuable inside. If they wanted a toy from the happy meal they could've always have gone to the local yellow arches to retrieve one instead of destroying my birdhouse!

As a geocache owner, one of the things that you have to make up your mind about is how you're going to react to a situation like this. You could decide to pack it up and quit saying to yourself, "that's it! I have done everything I can to be a part of this sport!" I have thought about this a few times before but have always decided to continue on and make geocaches and place them properly for others to find. I refuse to let the muggle get me down!

There's some who have asked me for advice on creating and placing their own geocache. Some of them after they have only found a couple! I always tell them that in my opinion, they should wait until after they have found 100 geocaches or so first. Many of them look at me funny as to why they would need to wait but invariably they realize later that they should have found more before trying to hide their own. This is something that is true pretty much across the board in any discipline.

A novice has some knowledge and makes a determination that the amount of knowledge they have acquired is sufficient to not necessarily be an expert but that it is enough to be competent. While I am all for new geocaches being placed and created, I believe it is vital that they are done properly and in accordance with the Geocache Listing Requirments/Guidelines as set forth by Geocaching.com.[33] Let me mention at this point that there are other listing services for geocaches but I have settled fully on Geocaching.com so all geocaches referenced pertain to that service.

There is an interesting aspect to geocaching known as a trackable. Trackables come in three forms: the travel bug, the geocoin, and the path tag. The reason that I put these in the chapter on disappointment is because all three of these items are supposed to be either be moved from geocache to geocache or in the case of the path tag they have some collectible value to them. They are "trackable" in that they have a trackable code on them.

The first time I learned about the travel bug was when I found a small toy Jeep in a geocache and around it was a dog tag. The dog tag had information on it that stated that it was a trackable item and it was not to be kept but to be moved to another geocache. My first reaction was, "this is cool!" so I followed the directions on the tag and I logged it on Geocaching.com and then I moved it on to another geocache. Just like it said.

Unfortunately, not everyone follows the rules. This was an early lesson in disappointment that I learned after getting more into this great sport. I bought a few travel bugs and attach them to a couple of items. One was a small Winnie the Pooh which I then sent on its way with its mission. Many travel bugs have a mission associated with them. Some missions are just to travel around from cache to cache but some missions are very specific.

For our Winnie the Pooh, its mission was to travel to all of the different Disney theme parks in the world. It seemed like a cool mission, right? We were disappointed when our Winnie the Pooh traveled aimlessly for several months and then finally disappeared off the map! Needless to say, it did not make it to any of the Disney theme parks.

So, what is your reaction to the situation? Do you give up or do you decide to continue to put out travel bugs with the knowledge that many of them may not make it to their final destination or complete their mission? Many people just quit putting out travel bugs and that is understandable but again that is a choice that you need to make with the knowledge that I have just given you. Sometimes, the travel bug makes it to the goal you set for it and that is a cool thing indeed.

The other item that you might find in a geocache is a geocoin. The geocoin is also an item that is trackable and it also may have a mission associated with it. I have only found a couple of these "in the wild" but I did what you're supposed to do which is to move the coin along according to its mission.

With travel bugs, sometimes the mission is written out and attached or included which I think helps it not get taken or lost as often in the process of getting to where you want it to go. This is more difficult for a geocoin because new geocachers are unfamiliar with the fact that they have an owner that is wanting it moved from cache to cache. Pretty much every geocoin I've ever seen is cool looking and is a temptation to those that do not understand that they are not to be kept.

However, the path tag is an item that has a trackable code that is normally meant to be kept by the finder. I really like path tags! The fact that it has a trackable code might confuse people into believing that either it needs to be moved along or that when they find a travel bug or geocoin that it is like a path tag and can be kept. Know the difference between the three of these and you will avoid disappointments down the road.

CHAPTER SIX

PLANNING

When we first started geocaching, our planning consisted of simply going to the website finding a cache or two nearby, printing them out, and then going out to find them. Back in 2006, there were only two ways to prepare to find a geocache: you could download them directly to your GPSr which was tricky for those that were not technology savvy or you could do what we did and print out the geocaches.

I think that on a good day we found seven geocaches and at the time we felt like we were very successful. Now don't get me wrong. For us, going fast and finding a large number of geocaches in a day was never the point. This is a topic that I cover in a different chapter.

Even from the beginning, we found geocaches while we traveled. This seems like a natural occurrence for geocachers. Planning back then consisted of looking at the Geocaching.com website for geocaches along the route we were going or geocaches around where we were going to stay. This provided us with two new aspects to geocaching.

The first is what is referred to as "geocaches along a route". Geocaching.com or another awesome geocaching utility website called project – gc^{34} will help you plan for finding these types of geocaches.

The second was to look for geocaches around our destination. At first, this doesn't seem like a big deal planning-wise. After you geocache for a while, you will know exactly why this is important. If this is a location that you've never been to then this step is even more important. Some of the factors that go into your planning would include:

1. types of caches
2. difficulty and terrain
3. the size of the container

Geocache planning also spills over into another aspect of the geocaching experience and that is a number of geocaches you want to find in one day. Now Susan and I really love to geocache! Therefore, we factor that into our day and in some cases, that is our day! But for some people, especially those with a spouse, significant other or family member that doesn't like to geocache, this planning becomes crucial. Perhaps, the person you're with doesn't want to geocache all day or even part of the day. This becomes something that needs to be negotiated ahead of time as part of your planning.

As some of my friends have done, they have worked out times where they go geocaching by themselves or with other geocachers so as not to create conflict. This is a solution that may work quite well for you. Many of my friends who solo geocache have also worked out an agreement that they will geocache some with their favorite muggle in exchange for doing something that the other person likes to do. For them, hobby-negotiating has become not only a science but an art!

Once you have geocached for a while you start to get better at planning especially in the area of time it takes based on the difficulty and terrain of the geocaches. Recently, Susan and I were trying to get to 1000 geocaches found. We were out of town in a location that we have never been before and we were planning that day to go back home. Also, the weather indicated that rain was on the way. This was one of the few days in our geocaching life where we had a numbers goal.

Our planning therefore for that day took a completely different turn. This is something else to think about and that is one planning day may be completely different than another planning day. We were able to successfully weave our way through town picking up what is referred to as "park and grab" geocaches. We dodged a few raindrops along the way and a few unforeseen obstacles and DNF's. We even managed to get a nice lunch and then hit the road before the rain really came down.

Sometimes, you might want to let the planning be done by someone else. One of the best ways to utilize this is with a GeoTour, GeoTrail, Power Trail or Geoart.

GeoTours (or GeoTrails) are a "tour" of a destination through a series of geocaches that are set up by an organization or individual. There are a wide variety of tours all over the world. In fact, many state and local tourism boards have discovered how geocaching can enhance a tourist's experience though GeoTours or GeoTrails. Each GeoTour or GeoTrail is unique and often provides an entertaining and deeper understanding of the area or destination where they are located. Some will have specific themes while others will have prizes at the end for finishing the entire tour.[35]

Susan and I have done three GeoTours so far and plan to do as many as we can! I think there are several appealing aspects to them including swag, unique destinations, and a sense of accomplishment.

Most GeoTours and GeoTrails have some kind of "passport" where you fill in various requirements such as getting a letter or keyword off the geocaches and then at some point when you have either finished the tour or built up enough points then you can either mail it in or deliver in person the passport to the local Chamber of Commerce or Visitor's Bureau. When you do, you might get a coin or path tag or perhaps some other items like a pen or maybe some discount coupons.

The GeoTours we have done so far all had a theme of some kind. Many times, they took us to historical areas and sometimes these areas are not on the popular tourist lists for that area. I really like these! They may not be glitzy or flashy spots that the usual tourist wants to see but that doesn't mean they should be missed.

Take the time to learn the local spots that they want you to see. Buy from the local shops. Eat at a non-chain restaurant that is often times listed in the passport or associated website. The person or organization that set up the GeoTour brought you to that spot so let them be a guide for you and take inspiration from their suggestions.

GeoTrails, as I am defining them in this book, are almost identical to a Geotour but are not directly linked to Geocaching.com. Don't let that in any way deter you from doing a GeoTrail! All of WVTim's fabulous gadget caches fall into this category.

A Power Trail is a set of consecutive caches along a route that allows cachers to find a large number of caches in a small amount of time and distance. They are usually placed right at or just over the 528 feet limitation from the previous and next cache. The difficulty and terrain levels are kept low to increase the ease of finding the containers.[36]

Geotour, Geotrail, Power Trail and Geoart teach great life lessons like perseverance and setting a goal and working hard to completing that goal. Many times, we need to be stretched and these can give us a good healthy challenge.

Whether it is walking or running further than we have before or in geocaching maybe we try to find more geocaches in a day that we ever have before. Set some more challenging goals for yourself! Strive to accomplish something you never thought you could do and if you don't succeed then pick yourself up and try harder the next time! It's your life but I would suggest you "grab the bull by the horns" and don't let go!

CHAPTER SEVEN

HEALTH

Getting Outdoors

STUDIES CONFIRM STRESS IS CAUSED BY NOT GEOCACHING ENOUGH

memegenerator.net

There have been some scientific studies that have shown that getting outdoors reduces stress. One study found that "those who lived in the areas with the most amount of green space had lower levels of cortisol, and their self-reported feeling of stress were lower than those who spent more time in urban settings."[37] Now, I know what you're saying, "I just can't get to that many green spaces". That's okay. Geocaching has other ways to improve your health!

This next section was provided by Sarah Murphy. Sarah has an unbelievable blog that you must put in to your reading list on a weekly basis! Thank you, Sarah, for letting this health article be included in the book! The blog and this article can be found here:

https://thegeocachingjunkie.com/

Geocaching is Good for You: 8 Reasons Why

"Go outside and play!" How many times did we hear that as kids? It seems our parents were definitely on to something, as the health benefits of being outdoors are varied and wide-reaching. But being close to nature is not the only thing that geocaching has going for it, with going to events and solving puzzles also having great rewards.

I had a look at what some experts had to say about various activities that are part of geocaching and I made a list of 8 ways geocachers benefit from their hobby.

1. Boosts Immunity

Since 2004, the Japanese government has invested millions of dollars researching *shinrin-yoku,* or *forest-bathing*. The idea is to reap the health benefits of being close to nature and walking through a forest. Researchers[38] brought middle-aged business men in to the forest outside Tokyo for twice-daily hikes over a period of three days and found that the activity levels of 'natural killer' cells (NK cells) increased by 56% after day two. NK activity was used as, "an indicator of immune function, particularly as an indicator of anticancer activity."

So the next time someone looks at you funny for saying you're going geocaching, just tell them you're practicing the Japanese therapy of *shinrin*

yoku instead

2. Relieves Stress

The research team also measured levels of cortisol (the stress hormone) in the subject's saliva and found the levels significantly lower in the forest environment. Even proximity to green spaces in more urban areas[39] can result in lower stress levels, meaning just a walk in a local park to pick up some caches can help you relax.

3. Taps in to your Creativity

Psychologists at the University of Utah and the University of Kansas found that being in touch with nature[40] made subjects scores on a creativity test soar. No wonder then, that there are so many creative caches out there!

4. Improves Memory

Doing a variety of puzzles can be very beneficial to your mental health. A US Study of older priests and nuns found[41] that subjects who undertook diverse cognitive activities, including reading a newspaper and doing puzzles were 47% less likely to develop Alzheimer's disease.

The Geocaching Junkie

5. Boosts Mental Health

A 2010 study[42] funded by the *National Institutes of Health* in the US measured various factors including diet, supplements, and exercise and found that cognitive training was most closely linked to a decreased risk of mental decline. If you feel like you're not getting anywhere with puzzle caches, at least you're giving your brain a workout

trying to solve them! Every cloud

6. Gets You Moving

I don't need to refer to any studies on the health
advantages of exercising; the benefits are well
known and plentiful. If you need extra motivation
to get outside and get moving (and I know I do!),
just make a geocache your reward at the end and
you'll be in better shape before you know it,
reaping the rewards including reduced risk of heart
disease and strengthening of bones and muscles.

7. Promotes Eustress

Eustress[43] is a type of 'positive' stress that you get
when you do something you find fun, like riding a

HIDE AND SEEK · 73

roller coaster or driving a go-kart. Assuming that you go geocaching because it makes you happy, then chances are the thrill of making the find is releasing eustress, which is really important to stay mentally happy.

8. Reduces Symptoms of Depression

Researchers at University College Dublin[44] found that "going out for coffee or chatting with a friend can reduce the symptoms of depression." Just in case you needed another excuse to attend that geocaching event!

I recently read this article[45] about Mark, who found that geocaching helped him through depression. Given the benefits to mind and body listed above, it's little wonder Mark attributes geocaching to keeping him "fit and grounded."

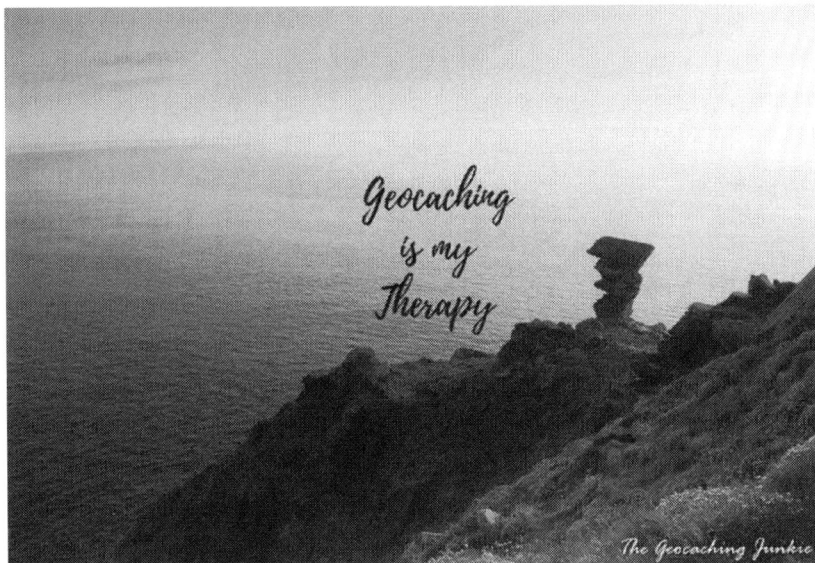

Geocaching is my Therapy

The Geocaching Junkie

The next time someone asks you 'what's the point?', be sure to tell them all about the benefits of our awesome hobby. Is there such thing as a healthy obsession? I think geocaching proves that there is![46]

Walking

Other than a few unique geocaches, you're probably going to have to walk to most of them. For every 2,000 steps more per day a person took at the start of the study, they had a 10 percent lower risk for heart disease in subsequent years. And for every 2,000 steps per day increase during the study period, the risk of heart disease fell an additional 8 percent, the researchers found.[47]

There is one study that actually ties walking in with something like geocaching and they came to this conclusion based on the results of this study:

Exercise induces chemicals that protect brain cells, or exercise is simply a marker for an overall healthy lifestyle, or there is **some positive interaction among exercise, healthy lifestyle and intellectually stimulating activity**. (Bold added)[48]

What does the evidence show? Surprise, surprise: walking is good for you and enacts multiple beneficial changes in our bodies. To name a few:

Kids who walk to school are fitter than peers who do not. Older healthy adults who walk briskly live longer than those who don't. Healthy adult males who engage in short bouts of brisk walking experience lower resting blood pressure and postprandial triglycerides. Regular walking improves working memory in older adults. Walking improves longevity in women over 70 years of age. Walking programs improve cognitive ability in people with Alzheimer's.[49]

One thing that I do not look forward to every week is getting on the treadmill. I know that it is good for me but I would prefer to be geocaching and not just scampering like a rat in a cage but some days this has to suffice. One thing I do is turn on the TV and that does help but I do not walk as far as I would if I were outside and more importantly walk with a purpose or goal in mind.

Over the last three years, I have been doing Weight Watchers® and by making this lifestyle change I have lost 100 pounds. Along with that, Susan and I have done a lot more geocaching during that time and that has also been an important factor in my weight loss.

One weekend, we went to the Lost Maples State Natural Area near Kerrville, Texas. We were there to enjoy this beautiful place and of course to do some geocaching. This was before I had lost my weight but while we were there we decided to hike out into the park and also decided we needed to go out and get Cache That Monkey (GC2JZK3) and then walk back.

As you can see from the photo, you know why the geocache has that name! From this angle, it looks just like a monkey. Such a cool rock formation!

When we figured out the distance out to the "monkey" and the geocache and then back again it was over 3 miles! Which was a lot for me back then. I can tell you right now that I would never have walked that far had it not been for geocaching. There was a goal that I needed to reach. There was a destination and it drove me to that location.

"I think many of us can benefit from having something tangible to get us to a location and to get us out moving because for me I can tend to be very sedentary. I need an incentive! In the past year, I have used geocaching to get me moving more that I had in the past.
Another interesting fact about getting off the beaten path and geocaching is that when you get onto uneven ground that causes you to really pay attention to where you are walking, it actually helps your brain. A walk in the park may soothe the mind and, in the process, change the workings of our brains in ways that improve our mental health, according to an interesting new study of the physical effects on the brain of visiting nature."[50]

"Walking at a good pace also has health benefits. "There's solid evidence that aerobic fitness ups the odds of living longer. Research suggests that just 30 minutes a day, five days a week can keep you fit."[51]

CHAPTER EIGHT

PROBLEM-SOLVING

So, at this point, you have decided to try geocaching. Awesome! As you go out looking for your first geocache, you run into a problem. You can't find it! So now what?

What you do next will ultimately determine whether you stick with this sport or not. Many people quit too early and that's a shame. Until you have some experience geocaching, there will be some geocaches that will not be easy.

One of the benefits to geocaching is the benefit of exercising a muscle that many times gets overlooked. No, I'm not talking about your biceps or triceps but that muscle that I'm referring to is your brain doing problem-solving. The good thing about exercising this particular muscle is that it can help you in normal day-to-day life as well.

There are many techniques that geocachers learn over time to use that helps them find a geocache. Probably the first place everyone will look other than around them is the cache description. Now, for the moment, I am going to focus on traditional or multi-cache geocaches.

Some of the time, the geocache description can be very helpful. Read it one more time and then read it again! You will be surprised that even though you read it carefully you still missed something.

Read the name of the geocache again. There may be a clue as to where the cache is there. Of course, many of these techniques do translate over to say puzzle caches as well. Remember, you are solving a puzzle every time in a sense even if it is a traditional geocache.

You can look at the hint that is given but sometimes there is no hint or it is not clear because the cache owner did not want to give away too much information. But, sometimes it is very helpful to aid you in your search so use the hint if you want to but that is totally up to you. The level of help that you seek is really up to you. This is another great thing about geocaching.

Another step you can take is to read the last several log entries on Geocaching.com. Now some of these areas get into what many people call spoilers (kind of like watching too many previews for a movie before the movie comes out). Again, that is completely up to you and your decision as to what you need to use to problem solve a geocache. There can be some excellent information provided by others that may not have been given originally by the cache owner.

Also, you can look at the photos on the cache page. Now, these can be real spoilers! So again, let the buyer beware. I have known geocachers when finding a geocache have placed within their photos a clue as to where the geocache is located without giving away all of the information as to where it is hiding. Now, I think that is a very clever thing to do. It preserves some of the need to look harder but it can at least give you a push in the right direction.

Nowadays, you can phone a friend or text a friend who has either found the cache or possibly is the cache owner if you happen to know them. I have used this method a few times and I have also been the person on the other end giving out the clues to the person who is searching for a geocache. One thing that I always do, is to ask them how much information are you looking for in this situation. Are you at your wits end or are you just looking for a little hint? I want to be able to preserve their hunt to the level that they want it preserved.

Puzzle caches are a different matter and this book is not designed to go into detail about how to solve a puzzle cache. There are some great resources available that I will add in the appendix section. The one thing I will say about puzzle caches in regards to problem-solving is that many of them can really stretch your problem-solving muscle and I highly recommend that you do some puzzle caches that really make you think.

Ironically, you may benefit from that muggle that is with you by asking them to help you. "While it is obviously helpful to involve people, who are more knowledgeable about the issues involved in a problem, sometimes non-experts can be equally, or more valuable. This is because they do not know what the 'common solutions' are, and can, therefore, tackle the problem with a more open mind and so help by introducing a fresh perspective."[52]

Another problem-solving technique that I like to use is what I like to call the "eye-opener" technique and that is to step back maybe sometimes even several feet back, close my eyes and then count to three and then opened my eyes again and give the location a "fresh look". Take a deep breath and ask yourself, "now where would I hide the geocache"? Then, I start by looking in that location.   From there, I would then search in a spiral pattern outward at the most likely and sometimes unlikely locations. As always, remember that some geocaches are missing so always keep that in mind as well.

CHAPTER NINE

NOT ALL WHO WANDER ARE LOST

You know how I said that I was not going to be doing home movies in this book? Maybe to be more accurate I should've said I'm not going to be doing a lot of home movies. I do, however, want to use some of the geocaches we have found as examples and lessons that we have learned.

One thing that I am not going to do is spoil or ruin any active geocaches. Any details that I give will either be of my own geocaches, archived geocaches, or geocaches where I have the owner's permission to share details about the cache.

The best example to date of where geocaching can take you is a geocache we found back in 2006. I went back and looked and it was the 10th cache that we had ever found! That alone should indicate how great of a geocache this was that it is still one of my best stories of where geocaching can take you. It is archived, sadly, but the story and the experience will live on.

The name of the geocache is "Chouteau Lock #17" (GCJ11E). The cache was hidden on 03/27/2004. It was archived on 07/12/2015 after being found 95 times and DNF five times. Here are a few pictures from the cache page:

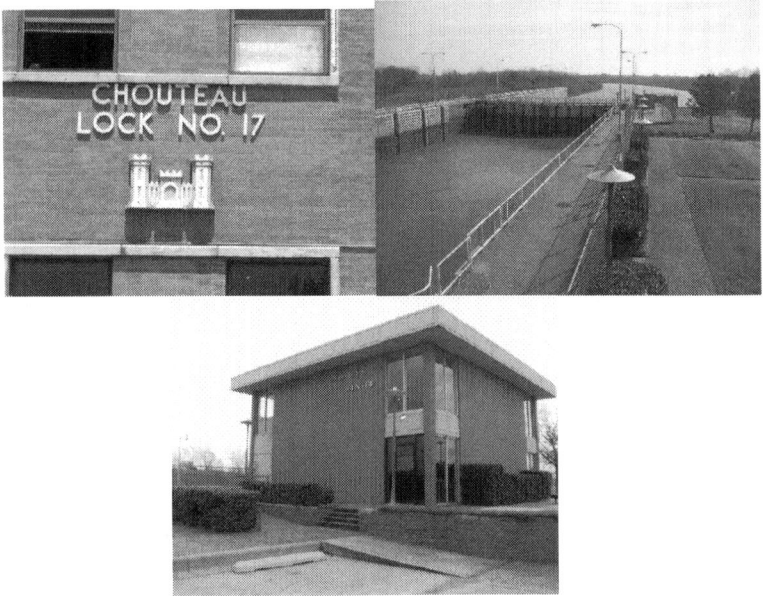

Here is our log from the geocaching website:

07/21/2006 My kids loved this place, who would have thunk it! We did too! Nice spot, we stuck around and watched the locks open and close for one small boat.

Not bad for our 10th log! We really hadn't at this point learned that the geocache log has two main purposes:

The first is to provide the geocache owner with insight into a geocacher's experience at their cache. Something that today I would say many if not most geocachers fail to understand. I think that they forget just who reads these logs. For most, it is a self-centered approach to the geocache log.

The second is the next geocacher or the next few geocachers who come by or who might read the log ahead of time in making a determination as to whether this is a geocache to go after.

Now back to the story. So, we were traveling through Oklahoma, and doing some hiking and teaching about history. Susan homeschooled all three of our sons and was very successful doing it. We used many of our trips as teaching moments for our school. This was one of those times. The funny thing about it is that we hadn't planned for it to be a teaching moment but we were always ready to seize the opportunity.

Here is part of the cache description:

This cache is located next to the Visitors Center at Chouteau Lock #17, east of US 69 and north of Muskogee. This is #6 in the series of caches along the McClellan-Kerr Navigation Channel. Eventually, this series will run all the way to the Oklahoma-Arkansas State Line. These caches will be placed mostly in parks along the waterway. The cache container is a hide a key box. The contents are a Coin, Log Sheet, and a pencil. Please trade the coin for another unique coin and sign the Log Sheet.

Make sure you tour the Visitors Center. They have a lot of good displays and a big window to watch the Barges go through the Lock. Good Luck and Happy Hunting. Here's a little History and Waterway Facts: The Navigation system begins at the Mississippi River mile 599 (599 statute miles north of where the Mississippi River meets the Gulf of Mexico). Keep in mind these are 'river' miles and that the distance would be much less if the river was not so tortuous.

The Navigation System is numbered by statute miles. The system is 445 miles long and crosses Arkansas, ending at the head of navigation called The Port of Catoosa. Let's begin our discussion about the McClellan-Kerr system by starting at the Port of Catoosa, mile 445 (Catoosa, Oklahoma) and work our way down to the Mississippi.

Will Rogers was once quoted as saying the Arkansas river would be "easier to pave than making navigable." The third longest river in the nation and the second most destructive, the Arkansas has long been tamed to create the world's most inland port in Catoosa, Oklahoma.

Senators John McClellan and Robert Kerr from Arkansas and Oklahoma, respectively, were the congressman responsible for bringing the system to completion in 1971. The system is a 445 mile stretch of water that drops 420 feet as it crosses northeast Oklahoma and the state of Arkansas.

There are 17 locks (some with dams) along the waterway that allow for flood control, hydropower, water supply, recreation, wildlife conservation and navigation. The locks each measure 110 feet wide and 600 feet long and are designed for 8 barges and a towboat. The depth of the locks varies from 14 feet for 54 feet. It can take 20 minutes just to be lowered in the lock. The doors only take a few minutes to open and close.[53]

This is a very well-written geocache description wouldn't you agree? It almost reminds me of an EarthCache. The funny thing about this one is that for us we had not read the cache description. I just made note of the fact that there was a geocache here on our way to somewhere else. When we arrived, we were amazed at what we found.

First, we had to find the geocache. I mean that was the initial reason why we came here. The funny thing about this one and this actually happens to many people is that the geocache was nothing special. It was a Nano underneath a metal bench. It was our 10th find and for us, I think that was kind of impressive since we really hadn't seen more than one of those at this point and I'm also sure that Susan found it. I'm sure I have noted before that she is, by far, the best geocacher in the family although Josh would disagree.

After we found the geocache, we went into the visitor center and looked around. We were impressed by the fact that this was even here. We really had no idea that there was a lock system in

Oklahoma and perhaps you did not know that either? We were looking around at the pictures of boats and some quite large ships that squeeze their way through this lock system. Our timing turned out to be fortuitous as after a few minutes being there a small fishing boat came up to this lock.

So here we were up in the visitor center observation deck and we were treated to a show. The operator in the tower next to us proceeded to open the first gate of the lock allowing the boat to enter. Then the lock was filled with water and then opened again so that the fishing boat could continue on down the river. This is a great example of a geocache that for many is not that great but the location is everything.

The irony of this geocache is that for us it turned into an educational moment for the family and a new find for us. However, if you read the last log entry prior to the reviewer making an attempt to contact the geocache owner, you will read a different experience that someone had. Their log is this, "don't bother coming it's gone". This is the best example of why this book was written!

Interestingly, this geocacher ended up finding only one and then quit the sport. Perhaps, had they explored this area and taken in what was clearly in front of them they may have had an adventure instead of having such a narrow focus and as it turns out appears to have spoiled their experience with geocaching.

There are countless places the geocaching can take you and more than can be talked about in a book but my point for this chapter is to give you some insight into places that you might not think of that geocaching will provide.

Here is another unique example. We were on a trip up to the Kansas area and as one of our side treks, we decided to pop over to Missouri to get that state souvenir[54]. Geocachers have many different statistics and souvenirs that can be collected and one of them is getting a state souvenir. When you find a geocache in a state that you had previously not found a cache in you get a virtual souvenir on your geocaching page.

After we grabbed Missouri, we decided to go over to a location that had a virtual geocache that was the shared border of Kansas, Oklahoma and Missouri. Now we had no idea what we would find at that location. We assumed that there might be a little sign or something like that but to our amazement, there was a stone monument and a plaque on the ground.

Now here's the unique thing about this! To get to this location you had to go down a dirt road not too difficult to drive down but it was not labeled at all. In fact, we missed the turn and had to turn around to go back to find it. This cool location is really hidden! This is another example of the great places that geocaching can take you!

Now here's the really cool thing. There are thousands of these locations in the world just waiting for you to find them! Just think of the adventures you can enjoy that could be yours if you just take the time to geocache in places that you normally do not!

CHAPTER TEN

MAKE MINE A COMBO

In my opinion, one of the ways to really enjoy geocaching is to combine it with other sports and hobbies that you might have. I'm not saying that you have to do this but I think in the long run it is a way to enhance both of your interests or perhaps even more than two. Some examples would be hiking and geocaching, rock-climbing and geocaching, scuba diving and geocaching, or one of our favorite combinations, sightseeing, and geocaching.

For us and for other geocachers that we know, the geocaching vacation is a must-do. Whenever we can, we combine these two together which makes both even more rewarding. Remember, that this type of combination doesn't have to be lengthy or pricey. It may just be a short weekend getaway. Now, it could be cross-country extravaganzas so don't get me wrong that is also a possibility.

Being able to travel opens up new areas for geocaches that you have not found and it gets you into possibly other states or provinces or even possibly other countries depending on what part of the world you live in.

Whatever the excursion, make sure that you do some planning before you take off on your adventure (please see Chapter Six on planning). The type of planning that you may do will differ from the planning that I may do.

For us, the geocaching is important but often the location will lend itself to other things like shopping or learning a bit of the local history. One of our recent trips took us to Independence, Kansas. Part of the reason why we went there was twofold.

Susan is a fan of Laura Ingalls Wilder and her Little House on the Prairie series. One of the Little House on the Prairie museums is just south of town. It also happens to have a virtual cache there so as you see we were able to combine the visit with her other interest. Also, we met up with a fellow geocacher, Tamisha Sewell, who goes by the geocaching handle of "Geocache Her". We were able to do a couple of her geocaches (with no help from Tamisha) and after that, we found some geocaches together that neither of us had found before. She also took us to some of her favorites in the area (again she only gave us a hint when we were completely stumped).

Now for some people whose personalities do not lend themselves to meeting "a total stranger", this may be difficult. But let me challenge those of you who are apprehensive about doing something like this. Take a step of faith and meet other geocachers and enjoy the sport together with them. You will be amazed at the fun and fellowship that will occur.

Perhaps, the best step for you might be to attend a geocaching event instead so that you can get used to meeting other geocachers. My suggestion is to go to a local event first before going to a Mega Event. I think you will find that it is more difficult to meet and get to know some of your local geocachers at an event of that size.

Now don't get me wrong, I strongly encourage you to go to a Megaevent! We were able to attend Geowoodstock14er this year. Geowoodstock is for us in the United States one of the biggest events in the country. For example, in Germany, it may be a

Giga event that you may meet and interact with many who become friends going forward.

Whatever the situation, try to expand and stretch yourself. Broaden your boundaries and step out into areas that perhaps are uncomfortable for you and you may find that it was well worth it.

Now the issue for some is that either a significant other or portions of your family are not interested in geocaching. That does make things difficult. My advice to you is to get creative! You may have to negotiate which I think many who have this situation try to do. Walk that fine line of compromise and request that geocaching is included in the planning.

Now, I'm not saying that you're going to turn them into geocachers overnight but look for an angle. I have heard that some people combine their snuggle's interests such as a memorable location that they are interested in going to with a geocache nearby. I first heard the term "snuggle" from Sandy Portacio on the Podcacher podcast and I think it is a clever and inventive way of describing a family member, significant other or spouse that does not geocache! Instead of calling them a muggle, this term gives a more descriptive and more personal connotation to it.

Perhaps, they like to take a boat ride and they're willing to go to an island to geocache. They get the nice boat trip and you get to find a geocache that may have a higher difficulty or terrain rating. Everyone wins! Another possibility is to include a location that both of you can go to and temporarily part ways such as a park or a beach somewhere that gives everyone an opportunity to do something they want to do but still logistically makes sense for everyone.

The possibilities are endless! It may be a cruise or a bike ride or something as simple as a shopping trip. Be creative! Think outside the box! Work the angles and communicate to them that this is something that you really want to do and that with the proper planning everyone can be happy. As Ms. Frizzle would say, "It's time to take chances. Make mistakes. Get messy!"[55]

CHAPTER ELEVEN

LIGHTS, CAMERA, ACTION

There came a point in 2015 that I felt like I wanted to join the ranks of the podcasting world. For years, I had listened to several different shows and still do to this day but I wanted to contribute and be a part so I asked Michael Miller if he would be interested in taking on a co-host on the Cache and Release podcast.

After considering the idea, he agreed and I joined the show as a co-host. The show was a lot of fun to do and when Michael decided it was time to put the show on hiatus, I decided I would strike out on my own. Geocache Talk was born and hopefully, the show has been fun, entertaining, and informative each week.

Recently, I was asked to write a review, for "Treasure" a movie written and directed by Chris Williamson. The movie has within it several themes that play into the title of the movie and each character's search for "treasure". One of the themes that is prominent in it is geocaching and I was pleasantly surprised and thrilled to see that it was integral and very front and center in the movie. Portraying geocaching in the way that it did makes me very glad and it showed that this idea of adventure is something that many people share and that it can be conveyed in such a meaningful way.

Geocaching in the media is not a new marriage. Podcacher, a weekly podcast which I love, has been around for a decade. They have done over 580 shows and are still going strong. It was an honor this past summer during Geowoodstock 14er in Denver to have the media table next to them.

Other podcasts are out there and are listed in the Appendix. Recently, Geocaching.com started their own podcast. Since there currently are no TV, radio, or movies for geocachers to enjoy until Treasure comes out in 2017, podcasts, vlogs, and blogs have filled the void for many.

The vision for my podcast was to discuss and promote geocaching with a weekly guest in an interview type format to accomplish that goal. It has been a fun ride so far and I hope that each week I can continue to elevate our great sport higher and bring to light the joy and adventure that awaits everyone.

Recently on the show, we did what I called a Podcast of Hope. The eight-hour marathon podcast that we did was for charity and was a huge success raising over $1000 for St. Jude's Children's Hospital. The format that I chose mirrored the format that I use on a weekly basis which is to have a guest on the show and then to talk about them, their experience with geocaching, and their passion for the sport.

Each of the eight hours that we did had eight separate themes and topics for each hour with different guests for each hour with a couple of exceptions where a few folks instead did a couple of hours. Some people asked can you do eight hours and still keep people's attention and I answered them, of course, I can I think I could go probably 24 hours but realistically, I think the next time I will try doing 12 hours.

I really like the format that I have chosen for the show because it allows for my listeners to not just hear me ramble on but it facilitates a richness and a uniqueness that each of my guests brings each week. It also allows for an insight into the diversity of the geocachers around the world. Another aspect that I'm able to do is to show the diversity of people that love this sport is much as I do.

There are a couple of different magazines published for the geocaching community but one that I particularly love is "FTF Geocacher".[56] Keith Petrus has done an excellent job putting together a quality bi-monthly magazine that has great stories, pictures, and tips from many contributors.

Another one is the UK Cache magazine. UK Cache Mag is a bi-monthly magazine, with all kinds of hints tips and articles about geocaching in the UK.

Surprisingly, there have been a good number of novels written with geocaching as the theme or subplot. A couple of fiction authors I want to point out are Michelle Weidenbenner and Russ Atkinson. Michelle has written to date a couple of great works in this area. One was called "Cache a Predator: A Geocaching Mystery" which is an award-winning novel and yes, Michelle knows she made a mistake on the burying a geocache mention but that aside it is a thrilling mystery that received wide acclaim.

She also wrote, "Eclair Goes Geocaching". A delightful children's book about Éclair and her grandmother, Stella, who invites her to go geocaching and the adventure is on! I really loved this book! I think it hit my childhood nature and it is right in my adventure wheelhouse as well.

Michelle also had some of her books made into trackables! I like that idea and I am going to do that with some of the copies of this book so if this is one of those books with a trackable code in it, please read it and move it along to another geocache!

Another geocaching author I love is Russ Atkinson. Russ is a former FBI agent that has written a series called the "Cliff Knowles Mysteries". So far, there are seven in the series but I know there are more on the way. "The Cliff Knowles Mysteries can be enjoyed by anyone who likes a good mystery novel, but geocachers especially enjoy the way he weaves geocaching into some of his books."[57]

In the appendix, I have included some vloggers, bloggers, authors, websites, and other resources for you. This list is not exhaustive but I've included some of my favorites.

Both of these authors don't know it, but they helped get me over the hump and get this book written. Perhaps these different authors, podcasters, movie directors, vloggers, and bloggers will inspire you to take a risk and step out of your comfort zone. I know they have done that for me!

"I've been absolutely terrified every moment of my life and I've never let it keep me from doing a single thing that I wanted to do." — Georgia O'Keefe

"Just don't give up trying to do what you really want to do. Where there's love and inspiration, I don't think you can go wrong." —Ella Fitzgerald

"Far and away the best prize that life offers is the chance to work hard at work worth doing." — Theodore Roosevelt

"What's money? A man is a success if he gets up in the morning and goes to bed at night and in between does what he wants to do." —Bob Dylan

"Build your own dreams, or someone else will hire you to build theirs." —Farrah Gray[58]

CHAPTER TWELVE

GIVING BACK TO THE SPORT

Finding geocaches isn't the only way to experience the adventure of geocaching. Another way that is overlooked by many in this sport is placing geocaches. Until you have planned and created your own great adventure for others to experience, I truly feel that your adventure is not complete. When you take the time to plan and to weave together your own adventure to present to the geocaching world, you are participating in the richness of the sport to a level that many geocachers sadly do not experience.

Now, I am not talking about hiding the great lamppost cache although some have elevated this often looked down upon hide by creating dioramas or utilizing an underground tunnel or placing the lamppost in a tree. There are some very creative geocache owners out there! What I'm referring to is the well-placed hide, the incredibly camouflaged container, the themed cache that brings a smile to your face and provides a story that you tell others.

When a geocache is hidden in such a devious and unique way, there is a story that is instantly built around it and each person that finds that geocache now has another page in their geocaching adventure story.

Let's talk about Gadget Caches. I first heard about these while perusing YouTube and noticed this guy, WVTim. Tim Eggleston aka WVTim points out that a Gadget Cache is a geocache that is easy to find but hard to open. In his videos, he shows you first what the geocache looks like and then what is cool about his videos is that the second half of the video shows you how he made it. If you've never seen any of these videos, you're really missing out! Take some time and go watch them!

Someone like WVTim has provided innumerable adventures on the grandest of scales over the years. His gadget caches provide that huge canvas that many geocachers look for so that they can paint that unique portrait that they are hoping they can create. When a well-placed and well thought through geocache meets an avid and thoughtful geocacher then there is a potential for a masterpiece to be created!

Even the tiny canvas often looked down upon, the lamppost cache, can make for an adventure. Many of you probably have not thought of the fact that a well-placed lamppost cache could be near a hotel and perhaps that geocacher that is staying there is needing your county to meet a challenge or just a way for them to complete a state. Maybe this person is not driving but is on a bus tour and they want to keep their geocaching streak alive and your lamppost cache has just made their day.

You see? The many variations of the canvas are needed. Now, don't get me wrong, we all want those coveted geocaches in our experience story. The gadget cache, that ammo can at the top of a mountain, that elusive cache that provides us with many retellings to others.

Take some time today and think through the kind of geocache that you enjoy and then take some steps toward creating that blank canvas for others. Find that spot that can provide the story that others can tell. A good geocache takes some sacrifice of time and energy from you but the reward is worth it and providing a chance for another person to learn a life lesson and have some adventure is priceless!

Another way to give back to the sport is to host an event. You can go to great lengths or just host a meet and greet at your favorite restaurant nearby. One of the events that has become an annual tradition for me is to host, The Great Hunt of Hunt County which I have mentioned is the name of the county we live in here in Texas. Here is an example of one of these events:

Geocache Description:

The Great Hunt of Hunt County 3: Pirates
Hosted by: Hunt County Geocaching Association
Location: Greenville, TX
Dates: February 27, 2016

We always welcome geocachers from all over and always welcome them as part of our HCGA family.

As always, there will be giveaways and door prizes!

Note: All the reservations and planning are in place so we will be ready for February 27th!!!

The caches are being redone out at this park for the event.
You will be able to get a souvenir that day!

Schedule

9 AM Registration and Check-in
9:10 AM Start caching!
12:30 PM Event ends with Door Prizes!

We had a great time and had a nice turnout even though the weather was a little chilly. We had great memories together and I loved watching everyone hunt for my hides that day!

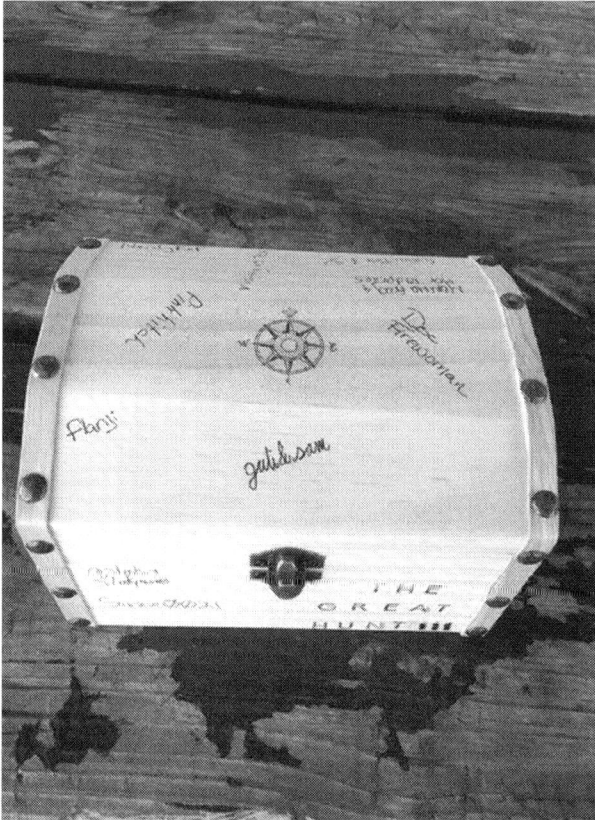

Some other cool things you can do to enhance the day is to give away some path tags or other types of geocaching swag. It can even be something as simple as giving out bug spray! Take lots of pictures and maybe even have a cool sign or prop that can be the event log like this one that we had for our pirate themed event.

CHAPTER THIRTEEN

DIGGING DEEPER

All of us who have geocached for some time remember the ones that mean the most to us so everyone's list is going to be a little different. What I want to do is point out some common denominators that I feel that everyone who is an avid geocacher agrees with about geocaching so that you get another accurate picture of why geocaching is the great sport it has become in almost every country of the world and is approaching 3,000,000 geocaches worldwide.

Of course, the first geocache of any quality will be high on everyone's list. Also, that very first quality find always holds a special meaning and a favorited milestone in a geocachers life. Our first find was in a historical cemetery in Marshall, Texas that had a lot of unique headstones and interesting history to read.

For me, the connection between history and treasure-hunting was really solidified that day and really drove home the connection for me with many geocaches that we have found since that day.

Most of us are blown away when you look at the map of geocaches in your area and realize just how many there are! For me, it reminds me of when Neo realizes what the Matrix is and that there is a whole other world out there that he didn't know existed! Things that are hidden and you walk by or drove by hundreds of times and never knew it was there and that is mind-boggling.

Another moment of excitement that I experienced was the first time that I realized that there were other types of geocaches that were available to be found. Seeing all the different icons that represent all these different types was incredible! Mystery caches and multi-caches and virtual caches made me realize that this sport had a richness that I never knew. On top of that, was when I realized that there was a category for the size of geocaches. Wow! What is a micro cache? How small can these things be?

I'll never forget the time that we were in Paris. No, not that Paris this was Paris, Texas and we had been searching for this geocache for a little while not having any luck. Susan found this electrical plate that she slid and voilà underneath it was the log which means that this electrical plate was fake and that it was actually the container! Well, my mind was officially blown!

The first time that I saw on YouTube one of those gadget caches by WVTim I mentioned earlier was his geocache called, "the key is the key", where you had to figure out how to open the lock for the geocache. All of these gadget caches really stand out and show why geocaching can be a joy not just for the geocacher finding the geocache but also for the geocache owner as he creates such a cool work of art! To give you an idea of some of the geocaches that Geocaching.com thinks are great, you should check out the geocache of the week.[59]

I have tried to avoid for the most part making this book a focus on my own geocaching hides but I do want to mention one of them and that is "Here Comes the Sun"[60] I adapted the idea after watching the movie, "National Treasure" which I mentioned previously.

When you get to stage one, you find a container holding a compass, a gnomon (the gnomon is the part of a sundial that casts a shadow), and a small plate with 4 color quadrants. In the morning hours, you place the gnomon in the center of the plate after you have lined up North using the provided compass and the shadow falls on one of the colors.

Each color has a set of coordinates and only one color takes you to the correct location for the final stage container. The other surprise is that there is no logbook but instead there are river rocks and a sharpie. You sign one of the rocks and return it to the container.

Now THAT is what I call an **ADVENTURE**!

WHAT OTHERS SAY ABOUT GEOCACHING

I wanted to give some of my friends a chance to tell what geocaching has meant to them. Here are some of their thoughts:

"One thing that we've learned over the 11 years that we've been producing our podcast is how Geocaching brings people together. The thrill of the hunt, the exploration, the intrigue and discovery of these little, hidden containers is something that is universal. It crosses boundaries and borders and can be understood in any language.

The community that has built up around geocaching is as close as your local Geocaching friends and as widespread as the players in other countries that you may never meet.

Our website and podcast has connected us with this worldwide audience and shows just how far and wide the appeal of "the hunt" has reached.

We look forward to sharing, even more, stories, connecting more people and making new friends as we play this "game". We hope to inform,

encourage and inspire people to stay safe and Keep on Cachin'!"
Sonny and Sandy of PodCacher
The World Famous, Longest Running Podcast about Geocaching

"What's so great about geocaching? For me, a lot actually. At first, it was a great way for me to get out and explore the city where I live. I found so many great out of the way parks and made my way into every corner of the larger recreation areas around town. I know where a lot more places are now because I have found a geocache near there. I have also started biking, not just for the exercise, but for a faster way to get to those bike trail geocaches!

Also, there's the thrill of the hunt and the fun of hiding geocaches for others to find. From a nice big ammo can in a lovely wooded spot to a particularly clever hide that has you scratching your head, nothing beats the feeling of making the find and signing the log. It is also very satisfying to read a good online log on a geocache that you put thought and effort into hiding. The geocaching map is ever changing and the challenge is limitless! So many places to explore, so little time.

After a year of geocaching, I started attending events. Why didn't I start sooner? The geocaching community is such a fun and friendly group! I have made some very good friends and now I have contacts for those phone a friend situations and have even been on geocaching road trips with people who love geocaching as much (or more!) than me.

My first geocache was found on a family camping trip. Now I make geocaching videos that document the fun times out on the geocaching trail with family members. Last summer in Colorado, I made a video that featured my 3000th find and I had seventeen family members with me for that milestone! I will treasure the experiences we have shared and the memories we have made for a lifetime.

By sharing my videos on YouTube and through social media, I have made geocaching friends all over the world! From weekly tweet chats, to facebook groups, to MEGA events and more, being part of the global geocaching community is a blast!

What's so great about geocaching? All these things and much more. See you on the trail... happy caching!"
Dan Buck, Geocaching with Darick

"We live in an amazing world, filled with beautiful places and clever people, and few things help us find both of those like Geocaching. We have been avid outdoors enthusiasts our entire lives, so once we learned about Geocaching it was a natural fit for us, as it is for many around the world. This global game allows the creative community of 'cachers to share wonderful places and unique ideas with strangers in a fun, social, and interactive way.

For us, Geocaching started as a curiosity, grew as a hobby, and has become a passion that has introduced us to many interesting people literally around the world, and brought us to innumerable places we might have never visited otherwise.

Regardless of whether you try it as an occasional family outing, or become an avid 'cacher, it's a game that is flexible enough to meet the interests of almost anyone who likes to get outdoors with any degree of a sense of adventure and curiosity.

However, you get out there, remember to cache safely, and cache often!"
The LANMonkeys

Geocaching: How I Learned to Stop Worrying and Love the DNF

It all started Christmas Day 2011 in the Eastern seashore town of Newburyport, Massachusetts. My brother-in-law Jason gifted me a Magellan eXplorist GC. I fumbled inserting the batteries and downloading GPX files of caches in the area. There were ten within a mile! From the first guard rail cache in the K-Mart parking lot, I was hooked on using billion dollar satellites to find Tupperware in the woods. As the game evolved, so did I as a geocacher.

Looking back at that first year I was a solo geocacher under the handle DannoBikes and was all about the numbers. I refused to find less than 5 in an outing or 20 in a week. I cached in hurricanes and blizzards. I dragged my oldest son Johnny only one at the time across the frozen streets of Boston in search of magnetic nano's stuck to stop signs and park benches.

The second year was when we moved to the suburbs and geocaching started to feel real. Real in the sense of getting lost in the woods, almost trampled by deer, stalked by coyotes, and plenty of ticks and poison ivy to last a lifetime. This was also a season in my life when I changed careers and working part-time gave me plenty of time to go caching. Numbers simply were not enough, I had to be the First to Find. An email would come across my iPhone and I would race off down back roads 20 mph over the speed limit taking a Honda Civic down dirt logging roads that even 4x4's would consider not traversing. I crossed swamps with Johnny on my shoulders using floating logs beavers chomped down as stepping stones. I bushwhacked 1 1/2 miles because it was faster.

By the third year, my wife had come to a crossroad join me in this cult of geocaching or never see me between sunrise and sundown. So, she joined me. The thrill of finding the cache first when we went out as a family or solving the puzzles that gave me nightmares was what attracted her to geocaching. We changed our handle to Team Pugatch to better represent who was out in the woods signing logs. When I wasn't geocaching, I was listening to one of a dozen podcasts eventually invited to be a guest on many of them.

The fourth year was the year I geocached the least. The desire was there, life just has a way of getting in the way. This was the year we launched our YouTube Channel: Get Lost! with Team Pugatch, and I spent most of my Monday nights as part of #USGeocachingHour on Twitter. Looking back at the first few days geocaching I knew I would surpass 1000 finds long before 5 years. I may have only made it to 675, however, each one was just as special as the first. Here's to the next year of geocaching, I know it's going to be a great adventure.

Danno Pugatch of Team Pugatch

"Geocaching has given me opportunities to see some beautiful places, learn quirky and unique history and make friends all over the world. What began for me as a part-time amusement has grown into a community of what I hope to be lifelong friends"

Debra Burris aka Docfirewoman

"Geocaching has impacted my life positively in so many ways. I have met some amazing people along the way and look forward to the adventure that lies ahead!"

Nic Hubbard, Cachly

"Geocaching has been a wonderful discovery for me. When I moved 12 hours away from the only place I really knew, I felt lost and needed my GPS just to find things like a grocery store and how to get back home. Little did I know, I would be using my GPS for so much more. Geocaching has given me a reason to get out and discover the new place I live. I found some awesome stuff already and even my boyfriend who has lived here all his life is finding new interesting places. We have met some amazing people through geocaching. I have made great friends in person and over the Internet, just because of this hobby I picked up for fun. Thanks Geocaching!!!"

Jamie 'Stardustzzz" Pullman

"My name's Jeff... but my secret code name is Anteaus. Okay, maybe my caching name isn't all that secret, but there's certainly a lot of people in my life that don't even know who Anteaus is or what he's about. When you find that first cache and many more after that, you feel like you're a covert operative of some sort, on a secret mission. It's thrilling, adventurous, albeit a little silly that you're looking for a piece of Tupperware, but there's this sense of mystery about the whole thing. Over time, the feeling that you are a secret agent may diminish a tad, but in its place, grows a

sense of community. You make a lot of friends when you get into Geocaching. Not only do you build friendships with your local Geocaching community, but with Geocachers from all over the world. The world is a big place, but Geocaching makes it feel a lot smaller!"
Jeff Arbaugh aka Anteaus

"Geocaching simply is finding hidden containers. But the more complicated explanation involves learning about GPSrs, coordinates, how to solve puzzles, and how to travel. It's adventures with new friends in urban and rural areas. The reward of geocaching isn't the geocache but it's the geocaching itself. And that's why I love it!"
Tom Brotherman aka Electric Water Boy

"Before I found out about geocaching, I often felt very anxious in social situations. I kept to myself and hated actually talking to other people. When I started attending geocaching events, I found out how fun they can be and how great other geocachers are. I got to know many of the local cachers in my area and I would now consider many of them my close friends. I even started hosting events; something I would have felt very anxious about before. Hosting events is now one of my favorite aspects of geocaching.

Eventually, I found geocaching videos on YouTube. I found out about many great new aspects of geocaching through the videos. I also found podcasts about geocaching. The internet is such a wealth of information! Through interacting with other geocachers on YouTube or Twitter, I felt like I had made many more friends, even though I hadn't actually met many of them. Luckily, this summer I had the chance to meet many of my internet friends in real life in Denver for this year's Geowoodstock. I am so thankful for all the amazing people I have met through geocaching.

One of the best things about geocaching is this: anywhere a geocacher goes in the world, they will always have friends there."
Sydney Sawyer aka Sherminator18

"My name is Christine Marie Chen aka Bayareaknitter in the geocaching world. I also use the name GeocachingBAK on social media, such as YouTube, Periscope, and Twitter.

If you had asked me what Geocaching was a couple of years ago, I might have vaguely blurted out "a worldwide treasure hunt!" Little did I know how much this activity would affect me and become a vital part of my life!

Unlike other geocachers, I can't really pinpoint the first time I actually heard about geocaching. I may have overheard someone mentioning it during a conversation. But I do know that my friend William, aka Revbeej, brought it back into light through Periscope. This led me to create my own geocaching account, download the app and take on a more enthusiastic look at the activity. After that, it seems to have quietly crept into my life and slowly progressed into a passion I can't live without.

On July 20, 2015, I found my very first geocache! I was surprised to see that there was one hidden only a few blocks away, in my own neighborhood. I'll never forget that cache! It was a sweet little birdhouse hanging on the corner of the cache owner's white picket fence, curbside! The perfect find for a newbie! I was in awe that there could be hidden treasures in plain site that I had never known existed! I longed to find more! But life got in the way, and I put it aside for a while, always keeping it alive in the back of my mind. As I look back today, I have no idea why I waited so long to search for my 2nd find. It didn't happen until I took a road trip to Oklahoma to visit my family.

It was April 4, 2016, while visiting my sister and her family in Oklahoma that I brought up the topic of geocaching. They had never heard of it either. To my surprise, my brother-in-law enthusiastically jumped up and said "Let's go!' My nephew downloaded the app and we all piled into their pickup truck and headed out on a family quest! We found 6 geocaches that evening in Moore, Oklahoma. I was hooked for life! The thrill reeled me in and I haven't looked back since.

During the first couple of months, it was more about the seek and find excitement. I felt a rush of adrenaline as I hunted for each cache. But as life has thrown me for a loop this year, it has taken on another role. It has become a necessary strand of thread that is holding me together. In a way, it's akin to therapy. When I'm feeling down and blue it gets me outdoors. As I breathe in the ocean air I forget about all my worries, if even for just a little while. As I focus on finding that little Tupperware container hidden under a stone in a quarry, my tension subsides. While crawling through a drain pipe, the stresses of the day melt away, as I see the light at the end of the tunnel. And as I emerge with travel bug in hand, all is well with my soul!"

Christine Marie Chen aka Bayareaknitter

ACKNOWLEDGEMENTS

Special thanks to Joshua Johnson, Darryl Wattenberg, Sonny and Sandy Portacio, Michael Miller, and all the other podcasters, vloggers, bloggers, and authors for taking me under their wings. They have been such an encouragement and blessing over the production of this book especially Michelle Weidenbenner for being my writing coach and mentor.

Also to the Motley Caching Crew and all my fellow geocachers that I have met over the years. You are great friends that have inspired me to be a better geocacher and a better person.

APPENDIX

Vloggers

The Geocaching Vlogger - https://www.youtube.com/channel/UCA0ptTLSLXK FsL4eOnF6RZg

Jamie Pullman - https://www.youtube.com/channel/UCjuTtSy7h1O NFWww777_Agw

Geocaching Kaity - https://www.youtube.com/channel/UCdS5izN7HKz pEepz2ZedziQ

Geohnny Cache - https://www.youtube.com/channel/UCxbBjdtUBhrL ui82JGGs9JQ

Geocache Her - https://www.youtube.com/channel/UCOs7IaRYTFii xOi7FbaEn0Q

The Geocaching Doc - https://www.youtube.com/channel/UCohEYY- VNCtGm0BnzU3o6fA

SoDak Zak - https://www.youtube.com/channel/UCyt9isB57cX0 LVRpKSgt54Q

Sherminator18 - https://www.youtube.com/channel/UCEflLQijoG6h MQEPkAP6neQ

Memfis Mafia - https://www.youtube.com/channel/UC3DfarWahnD 9MLN5VE3u6qg

Kennysart -
https://www.youtube.com/channel/UC79ET6-
aoOrZKsjBR-H2gYg
Oamaru Geofest -
https://www.youtube.com/channel/UCarixRnhCw1
drp3WSssN6gg
Geopaul -
https://www.youtube.com/channel/UCufcuCziCFJX
0_xiiAXD2_Q
scottinojaivideos (gsmX2) -
https://www.youtube.com/channel/UC-
QAD0G35uYFKedu1zorcMg
The Aussie Geocacher Seemyshells -
https://www.youtube.com/channel/UCUM4o-
5_UmcmJjqHa027baw
Neil Moore -
https://www.youtube.com/channel/UCNeMXICOws
I0WfSb3keHmkA
Lan Monkeys -
https://www.youtube.com/channel/UCZ_TIfLIQQMl
f03LkJo4Mgg

Podcasts

Podcacher - http://www.podcacher.com/
The Geocaching Podcast -
http://geocachingpodcast.com/
Geosnippets Reboot Podcast -
http://geosnippits.com/
Geogearheads - http://www.geogearheads.com/
Geocachetalk - http://geocachetalk.com/
Caching in the Northwest -
http://cachingnw.com/
Chicago Geocaching Podcast -
http://chicagogeocacher.com/

Geocaching.com podcast -
https://www.Geocaching.com/blog/podcast/

Blogs

The Geocaching Junkie –
https://thegeocachingjunkie.com/
Memfis Mafia -
https://memfismafia.wordpress.com/
Sherminator18 -
https://sherminator18.wordpress.com/
LanMonkeys Adventures -
http://lanmonkey.blogspot.ie/
Mad Cacher
http://www.madcacher.com/

Authors

Russ Atkinson -
http://cliffknowles.ackgame.com/
Michelle Weidenbenner -
http://michelleweidenbenner.com/
Cully Long -
http://www.puzzlecachepractice.com/

Resources

FTF Magazine – ftfgeocacher.com
UK Cache Mag - http://www.ukcachemag.com/
Cachly – cachly.com
#usgeocaching hour – tweet chat on Mondays
#ukgeocaching hour – tweet chat on Tuesdays

Geocaching puzzle of the Day –
geocachingpuzzleoftheday.com
Puzzle Cache Practice -
http://www.puzzlecachepractice.com/
Gadget Caches -
https://www.youtube.com/user/gadgetcaches
Ground Zero - http://geogz.com

Stores

I.B. Geocaching - http://ibGeocaching.com/
Space Coast -
http://spacecoastgeocachers.com/products
Drives Cache Closet -
http://www.drivescachecloset.com/
Landsharkz - http://landsharkz.ca/
Cache Advance - http://www.cache-
advance.com/
Coins and Pins - http://www.coinsandpins.com/

GLOSSARY OF TERMS[61]

ALR

"Additional Logging Requirement". Logging requirements beyond finding the geocache and signing the log. All ALRs must be optional for finders of a geocache.

Ammo Can

Ammunition boxes or ammo cans are containers originally designed for safe transport and storage of ammunition. Ammo cans are popular containers for regular or large geocaches.

APE Cache or Project A.P.E. Cache

In 2001, fourteen geocaches were placed in conjunction with 20th Century Fox to support the movie Planet of the Apes. Each geocache represented a fictional story in which scientists revealed an Alternative Primate Evolution. These geocaches were made using specially marked ammo cans and contained an original prop from the movie. Only one Project A.P.E. cache still exists today.

Archive

Archiving permanently removes a geocache listing from search results. A geocache owner can archive their own listing. A geocache owner cannot unarchive it. As an alternative to archiving, the geocache can be temporarily disabled if maintenance is going to be performed or the container will be replaced in the near future.

Attributes

Icons featured on a details page for geocaches that describe specific characteristics of a geocache. There are several classes of attributes, such as whether or not you need special equipment, possible hazards along the way, or unique conditions one should be aware of. Attributes can show whether or not a cache is wheelchair accessible, dog-friendly, requires a flashlight, and more. Attributes are also a tool to help you filter the types of geocaches you would like to search for when building a Pocket Query. More about Attributes here.

Basic Member

The introductory membership type for Geocaching.com. There are two types of membership, Basic, and Premium. Geocaching Premium Membership offers additional features that Basic membership does not provide.

Benchmark

Using your GPS unit and/or written directions provided by NOAA's National Geodetic Survey (NGS), you can seek out NGS survey markers and other items that have been marked in the United States. Check out our page about Benchmark Hunting for more details.

Bison

Also known as a "Bison tube". A small, metal, water-tight cylindrical container that can be used for micro caches. Its name comes from the original manufacturer, but there are now several other brands on the market.

Bookmark List

A Geocaching Premium Membership feature that can be used to group geocache listings in whatever way you like. You may want a Bookmark List of caches you intend to find this weekend or perhaps an "all-time favorite" list to share with friends.

Bug

Also known as a Travel Bug®. A trackable tag with a unique code that can be attached to an item. The trackable is then carried from cache to cache (or person to person) in the real world, and its progress can be followed on Geocaching.com. More about Travel Bugs and trackables.

BYOP

"Bring Your Own Pen/Pencil". An acronym often used by geocache owners to communicate to other geocachers that you will need to bring your writing utensil in order to sign the cache logbook.

Cache

A shortened version of the word geocache.

Cacher

Also known as Geocacher. One who participates in geocaching.

Caches Along a Route

A Geocaching Premium Membership feature that allows you to identify geocaches along a specific route for convenient geocaching.

Challenge Cache

A type of geocache that requires geocachers meet a geocaching-related qualification or series of tasks before the Challenge Cache can be logged online. Waymarking, Benchmark Hunting, and Wherigo-related qualifications or series of tasks also qualify.

Charter Member

Geocachers who bought a Geocaching Premium Membership the first year it was offered and every year since. Please thank any Charter Members you meet on the trail since the site would not be here today without them.

CITO

"Cache In Trash Out" is an ongoing environmental initiative supported by the worldwide geocaching community. Since 2002, geocachers have been dedicated to cleaning up parks and other cache-friendly places around the world. Learn more at www.Geocaching.com/cito.

Collectible

A status assigned to any trackable item that people can keep it in their possession, and do not have to physically move it to another geocache. Conversely, non-collectible trackable items can be easily grabbed, dropped, discovered, etc. More about trackables here.

Collection

A grouping or list of collectible trackable items that can be seen only by the owner. Trackables in a collection can only be discovered, and cannot be grabbed, dropped or dipped. Conversely, items in an Inventory can be seen by other geocachers and can be grabbed, dropped, discovered, etc. More about trackables here.

Coordinates

A pair of numbers (latitude and longitude) that pinpoint an exact position, or waypoint, on the Earth. Latitudes are horizontal lines on the globe that run parallel to the Equator (similar to rungs on a ladder). Latitudes never intersect, and one degree of latitude equals approximately 69 miles (111 kilometers). Longitudes (also called meridians) are vertical lines on the globe that converge at the North and South Poles. They are widest apart from each other at the Equator. The Prime Meridian runs through Greenwich, England near zero degrees longitude.

Creed, The

Also known as the "Geocachers' Creed". Designed to help orient new players to the ethos of the geocaching community and to guide experienced players in questionable situations, so that everyone can enjoy geocaching.

Datum

In the case of GPS, datums are different calculations for determining longitude and latitude for a given location. A datum is chosen to give the best fit given the true shape of the Earth.

Currently, Geocaching.com uses the WGS84 datum for all caches.

Difficulty and Terrain or D/T

Geocaches are rated in two categories, each designated on a 5-point scale (in half-point increments). Difficulty relates to the mental challenge of finding a geocache, while Terrain describes the physical environment. Therefore, a D1/T1 rating would be the easiest geocache to find, while a D5/T5 difficulty/terrain rating would be the most difficult. Our Geocache Rating System can be used to help set the rating for your geocache.

Dipping

The act of logging a trackable into a geocache, and immediately logging it back into one's possession. This registers miles traveled on a trackable. You can also achieve the same goal with a "Visit" log. More about Travel Bugs and trackables.

Disable

A status used to mark a geocache as temporarily inactive. A disabled geocache may need repairs or could be in an inaccessible area (construction, hunting, winter closures, etc...). This status is meant to be temporary and should be resolved within a reasonable amount of time.

DNF

"Did Not Find". An acronym used by geocachers to state that they did not find a cache.

EarthCache

An EarthCache is a special place that people can visit to learn about a unique geoscience feature of our Earth. EarthCache pages include a set of educational notes along with cache coordinates. Visitors to EarthCaches can see how geological processes have shaped our planet, how we manage its resources and how scientists gather evidence to learn about the Earth. Learn more at www.earthcache.org.

Event Cache

An Event Cache is a gathering of geocachers or geocaching organizations. The Event Cache page specifies a time for the event and provides coordinates to its location. Attending and logging an Event Cache increases your find count. See the full list of Geocache Types.

Find Count

The number of geocaches a player has found.

FTF

"First to Find". An acronym written by geocachers in physical cache logbooks or online when logging cache finds to denote being the first to find a new geocache.

GC Code

A unique identifier associated with every geocache listing. The GC Code starts with the letters "GC" and is followed by other alphanumeric characters, such as GCK25B.

Geocache

A hidden container that usually includes a logbook for geocachers to sign. Also known as a cache. However, there are currently over a dozen geocache types, each type being a different variation of the game. See the full list of Geocache Types.

Geocacher

One who participates in geocaching.

Geocaching

A real-world, outdoor treasure hunting game using GPS-enabled devices. Participants navigate to a specific set of GPS coordinates and then attempt to find the geocache hidden at that location.

Geocaching HQ

World headquarters of Geocaching.com, Waymarking.com, Wherigo.com, and Groundspeak. Located in Seattle, Washington, USA.

Geocoin

Geocoins work similarly to Travel Bugs®. They are coins with a unique code that can be attached to an item. The geocoin is then carried from cache to cache (or person to person) in the real world, and its progress can be followed on Geocaching.com. Geocoins are often created as signature items by geocachers and can also be used as collectibles. More about Travel Bugs and trackables.

Giga-Event

An Event Cache that is attended by 5,000+ people. These large events attract geocachers from all over the world and are often held annually. Note: A Mega-Event cache is attended by 500+ people.

GPS

"Global Positioning System". A system of satellites working with a GPS receiver to determine a person's location on Earth. More about geocaching with a GPS.

GPS Adventures Maze Exhibit

The GPS Adventures Maze is a traveling educational exhibit developed to teach people of all ages about navigation, GPS technology, and geocaching. A hands-on experience that features GPS technology (its history, current uses, and future possibilities), it simulates geocaching by leading visitors through a 2,500 square foot maze rich with interactive science experiences. While the GPS Adventures Maze has ended its run in the United States, geocachers wishing to experience this exhibit will still have the opportunity to do so in Canada and at Mega-Events throughout Europe.

GPSr

Slang for a GPS receiver. Equipment to receive GPS signals for use in navigation.

GPX (GPS eXchange Format)

A common GPS data format used to describe waypoints, tracks, and routes that can be interchanged between GPS devices and software.

Ground Zero (GZ)

The point where your GPS device shows that you have reached the geocache location. At ground zero, you are zero feet (or zero meters) away from your destination.

Groundspeak

Groundspeak, Inc. is the company that owns and operates Geocaching.com, Waymarking.com, and Wherigo.com. Groundspeak was launched in 2000 by Jeremy Irish, Elias Alvord, and Bryan Roth. The Groundspeak headquarters is located in Seattle, Washington, USA, and is referred to as Geocaching HQ.

Inventory

A grouping or list of non-collectible trackable items that can be seen by other geocachers. Trackables in an inventory can be grabbed, dropped, discovered, etc. Conversely, items in a collection can only be seen by the owner and can only be discovered (not grabbed, dropped or dipped). More about trackables.

Latitude

Latitudes are horizontal lines on the globe that run parallel to the Equator. Latitudes never intersect, and one degree of latitude equals approximately 69 miles (111 kilometers). The Equator is at 0 degrees Latitude and divides the Northern and Southern Hemispheres. Think of latitude as rungs on a ladder.

Letterbox(ing)

Letterboxing is another form of treasure hunting using clues instead of coordinates. In some cases, the letterbox owner has made their container both a letterbox and a geocache and posted its coordinates on Geocaching.com. If there is a stamp inside a Letterbox Hybrid, it is not an item intended for trade; the stamp is meant to remain in the box so visitors can use it to record their visit. More about Letterboxing.

LN

"Left Nothing". A common term used when a geocacher leaves nothing in the geocache and simply signs the logbook.

LOC

The original download format for the search results page on Geocaching.com.

Locationless (Reverse) Cache

A grandfathered cache type considered the opposite of a Traditional Cache. Instead of finding a hidden container, geocachers locate a specific object and log its coordinates. Locationless Caches are no longer supported on Geocaching.com but have evolved into Waymarking.

Lock & Lock

Lock & Lock (also seen as Lock 'n Lock or Locknlock) is a type of container that uses four snaps on the lid to create a seal. While used colloquially by geocachers, "Lock & Lock" is actually a specific brand of this kind of container.

Log

The physical record of everyone who has signed/interacted with a geocache.

Also, the online record of everyone who has interacted with a geocache.

Also, the online record of anyone who has interacted with a trackable.

Also, the physical logbook inside a cache is often referred to as a log.

Also, the act of recording a find, as in, "I am going to log this cache".

Additionally, online cache logs can record finds, DNFs, notes, suggest a cache needs maintenance, etc.

Logbook

A physical record of everyone who has found a geocache. Usually made of paper, logbooks come in many different sizes, shapes, and formats.

Longitude

Longitudes (also called meridians) are vertical lines on the globe that converge at the North and South Poles. They are widest apart from each other at the Equator. The Prime Meridian runs through Greenwich, England near zero degrees longitude.

LPC

"Lamp Post Cache". A common type of geocache hidden under an unsecured lamp post base.

Mega-Event Cache

An Event Cache that is attended by 500+ people. These large events attract geocachers from all over the world and are often held annually. Note: A Giga-Event cache is attended by 5,000+ people.

Micro

The smallest geocache size. Micros are about the size of a film canister, and sometimes smaller. Nanos (about the size of a pencil eraser) are a subset of Micros.

Muggle

A non-geocacher. Based on "Muggle" from the Harry Potter series, which is a non-magical person.

Muggled

The discovery of a geocache by a non geocacher. When a cache has been "muggled", it usually means it was dismantled or removed by an unsuspecting non-player.

Multi-Cache

A Multi-Cache involves two or more locations. The final location is a physical container. There are many variations, but most Multi-Caches have a first stage with a hint to find the second stage, and the second stage has a hint to the third, and so on. See the full list of Geocache Types.

Mystery Cache

A non-Traditional Cache type that doesn't fit into the other categories. Coordinates listed on the cache page are often bogus, and the final coordinates must be solved for through a series of steps or instructions. Also known as a Puzzle Cache. See the full list of Geocache Types.

Nano

The tiniest of all Micros—the smallest unofficial geocache size. Nanos are about the size of a pencil eraser.

Non-collectible

A status assigned to any trackable item that can be easily grabbed, dropped, discovered, etc. Conversely, collectible trackables are items that people can keep it in their possession, and do not have to physically move it to another geocache. More about trackables here.

Pocket Query (PQ)

A Geocaching Premium Membership feature, a Pocket Query is a custom geocache search that you can create and download on a daily or weekly basis. PQs give you the ability to filter your searches so you only receive information on the geocaches you want to search for in either a GPX or LOC format. This feature lets you download up to 1,000 caches at a time.

Power Trail

A path with a large number of caches placed within close proximity to each other. Promotes players' ability to easily increase their find count.

Preform

A plastic container similar in appearance to a test tube, but with a threaded neck. Normally formed into containers such as soda bottles by securing them into a mold then injecting them with compressed air. Preforms are durable and water tight, which makes them excellent geocache containers.

Premium Member

Geocaching.com members with a paid Geocaching Premium Membership. Premium members have more features available to them than Basic members.

Puzzle Cache

A type of Mystery Cache involving puzzles to be solved to determine the final coordinates. The puzzle should be solvable from the information provided on the cache page. See the full list of Geocache Types.

Reviewer

Community volunteers from all over the world who review geocaching listings for content and publish cache listings on Geocaching.com. Published geocaches must adhere to Geocache Listing Requirements / Guidelines.

ROT13

A simple letter substitution cipher, or code, where each of the letters are rotated 13 characters up or down in the alphabet. Hints for geocaches are encrypted using ROT13.

Decryption Key

A|B|C|D|E|F|G|H|I|J|K|L|M

N|O|P|Q|R|S|T|U|V|W|X|Y|Z

(letter above equals below, and vice versa)

Signal

Signal the Frog is the official mascot of Geocaching.com.

Signature Item

An item unique to a specific geocacher that is left behind in caches to signify that they visited that cache. These often include personal geocoins, tokens, pins, craft items or calling cards.

SL

"Signed Log".

Spoiler

A spoiler is information that can give details away and ruin the experience of something. For example, telling someone the end of a movie before they see it. In geocaching, a spoiler gives away details of a geocache location and can ruin the experience of the find.

STF

"Second To Find". The second person to find a geocache after it has been placed.

SWAG

"Stuff We All Get." Trade items left in caches by geocachers.

TB

"Travel Bug®". A tag with a unique code that can be attached to an item. The trackable is then carried from cache to cache (or person to person) in the real world, and its progress can be followed on Geocaching.com. Also known as Trackables and GeoCoins. More about Travel Bugs and trackables.

TB Hotel

"Travel Bug Hotel". A geocache with the intended purpose of acting as an exchange point for Travel Bugs. These are almost always regular or large sized containers. More about Travel Bugs and trackables.

TFTC

"Thanks For The Cache". An acronym written by geocachers in logbooks or online when logging cache finds. Occasionally written as T4TC. Side note: Please take time to write at least a few sentences when you log your find online. This how you say "thank you" to the cache owner for creating and placing the geocache.

TFTH

"Thanks For The Hide". Occasionally written as T4TH.

TNLN

"Took Nothing. Left Nothing". Usually written in geocache logbooks by geocachers who do not trade for material contents in a cache.

TNLNSL / TNSL

"Took Nothing. Left Nothing. Signed Logbook" / "Took Nothing. Signed Logbook".

TOTT

"Tools of the Trade". An acronym used for any of the tools that might be used to search for/retrieve/find/log a geocache.

Trackable

A tag with a unique code that can be attached to an item. The trackable is then carried from cache to cache (or person to person) in the real world, and its progress can be followed on Geocaching.com. Also known as Travel Bugs, TBs, and GeoCoins. More about Travel Bugs and trackables.

Tracking Number

A unique number associated with a Travel Bug or trackable. Tracking numbers are used as proof that a geocacher physically came in contact with an item. Tracking numbers also double as a way for users to locate the personal web page for a Travel Bug. More about Travel Bugs and trackables.

Traditional Cache

The original geocache type. The coordinates listed on the Traditional Cache page provide its location. Geocache containers vary in size, but must include a logbook or logsheet. Large geocaches generally include SWAG or trackable items for trade, while small "micro" caches may only hold a logsheet. See the full list of Geocache Types.

Travel Bug®

A trackable tag with a unique code that can be attached to an item. The trackable is then carried from cache to cache (or person to person) in the real world, and its progress can be followed on Geocaching.com. More about Travel Bugs and trackables.

Virtual (cache)

A grandfathered geocache type where geocachers discover locations rather than containers. The requirements for logging a Virtual Cache vary—you may be required to answer a question about the location, take a picture, complete a task, etc. In any case, you must visit the coordinates before you can post your log. These are still available to find, but no longer available for creation on Geocaching.com. See the full list of Geocache Types.

Watchlist

Lists that users maintain to receive notifications regarding specific geocaches and/or trackables. Users receive a copy of each posted log via email.

Waymarking

Waymarking.com offers a way to mark unique locations on the planet and give them a voice. While GPS technology allows us to pinpoint any location on the planet, mark the location, and share it with others, Waymarking is the toolset for categorizing and adding unique information for that location.

Waypoint

A reference point for a physical location on Earth. Waypoints are defined by a set of coordinates that typically include longitude, latitude and sometimes altitude. Every geocache listed on our website is a waypoint. Geocaching.com generates a unique GC code associated with every geocache listing.

Webcam Cache

A grandfathered geocache type using existing web cameras placed by individuals or agencies that monitor various areas such as parks or business complexes. The idea is to get yourself in front of the camera to log your visit, then use a smartphone or ask a friend on a computer to look up the website displaying the camera shot. You or your friend must save the picture in order to log the cache. These are still available to find, but no longer available for creation on Geocaching.com. New Webcam caches are now in the Web Camera category on Waymarking.com. See the full list of Geocache Types.

WGS84

The most current geodetic datum used for GPS is the World Geodetic System of 1984 (WGS84). The significance of WGS84 comes about because GPS receivers rely on WGS84. Geocaching uses the WGS84 datum by default. We also use the coordinate format HDDD MM.MMM, which is a standard for handheld GPS receivers. HDDD means Hemisphere and degrees. MM.MMM are minutes in decimal format. It is critical that the format be correct, otherwise geocachers will be unable to find your geocache.

Wherigo™ Cache

Wherigo.com is a toolset for creating and playing GPS-enabled adventures in the real world. By integrating a Wherigo experience, called a cartridge, with finding a cache, the geocaching hunt can be an even richer experience. Among other uses, Wherigo allows geocachers to interact with physical and virtual elements such as objects or characters while still finding a physical geocache container. A Wherigo-enabled GPS device or a smartphone running the Wherigo app is required to play a cartridge.

ABOUT THE AUTHOR

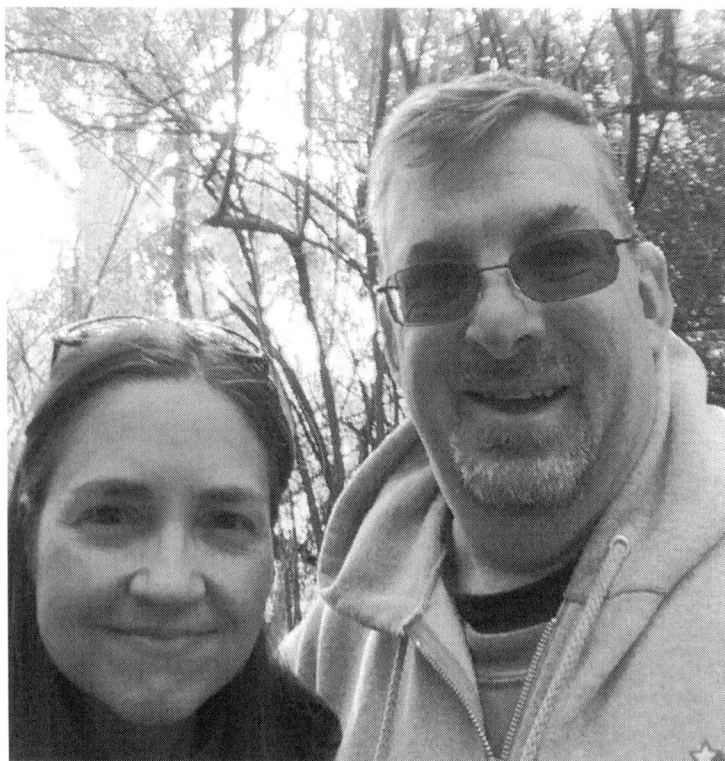

Gary and Susan Slinkard have been avid geocachers for over 10 years. They have found over 1,000 geocaches and have hid and maintain many near their home in Northeast Texas. Gary has a weekly podcast, Geocache Talk, where he interviews geocachers from all over the world.

END NOTES

1 http://www.dictionary.com/browse/sport
2 https://en.wikipedia.org/wiki/Geocaching
3 http://www.merriam-
webster.com/dictionary/adventure
4 http://headhardhat-
geocache.blogspot.com/2013/01/the-history-of-bison-
tube-why-is-it.html
5 http://www.sciencebase.com/science-blog/five-leaf-
clovers.html
6 http://www.oakislandbook.com/wp-
content/uploads/Readers-Digest-January-1965-
OakIslandsMysteriousMoneyPit.pdf
7 Whipps, Heather. "For Sale: Island with Mysterious
Money Pit". Retrieved 5 December 2005
8 Nickell, Joe (March 2000). "The Secrets of Oak
Island". Skeptical Inquirer
9 Nickell, Joe (March 2000). "The Secrets of Oak
Island". Skeptical Inquirer.
10 Forks, J.P. (August 20,
1857). "Correspondence". Liverpool Transcript.
Liverpool, Nova Scotia: S. J. M. Allen.
Retrieved January 26, 2014.
11 McCully, J.B. "The Oak Island Diggings." Liverpool
Transcript, October 1862
12 Phy, Paul "Oak Island - The Reasons for expecting
there is Treasure there." Yarmouth Hearld, February
19, 1863
13 Nickell, Joe (March 2000). "The Secrets of Oak
Island". Skeptical Inquirer.
14 Forks, J.P. (August 20,
1857). "Correspondence". Liverpool Transcript.
Liverpool, Nova Scotia: S. J. M. Allen.
Retrieved January 26, 2014.

15 "Response to the Oak Island Folly." The Novascotian, 30 September 1861

16 A Member. "A History of The Oak Island Enterprise." British Colonist (in 3 chapters published on 2, 7, and 14 January 1864)

17 DesBrisay, Mather Byles. "History of the county of Lunenburg". Internet Archive. Toronto: W. Briggs.

18 http://www.history.com/shows/the-curse-of-oak-island

19 Lord Carnarvon's description, 10 December 1922, quoted in: Reeves, Nicholas; Taylor, John H. (1992). Howard Carter before Tutankhamun. London: British Museum. p. 141. ISBN 0-7141-0952-5.

20 "Dallas Museum of Art Website". Dallasmuseumofart.org. Retrieved 18 July 2009.

21 http://mulubinba.typepad.com/ra_viewers_perspective_of/2011/04/thrors-map.html

22 https://en.wikipedia.org/wiki/National_Treasure_(film)

23 https://en.wikipedia.org/wiki/Archaeoastronomy

24 https://www.Geocaching.com/about/history.aspx

25 https://en.wikipedia.org/wiki/Geocaching

26 http://www.movemequotes.com/top-11-helen-keller-quotes/

27 https://en.wikipedia.org/wiki/Fire_ant

28 http://www.madcacher.com/geocaching-tips/geocaching-and-snake-safety/

29 http://www.madcacher.com/geocaching-beginners/geocaching-and-tick-prevention/

30 https://www.youtube.com/watch?v=6S1Uh3vJN7k

31 https://www.verywell.com/chiggers-pediatric-dermatology-basics-2633479

32 http://www.prevention.com/health/stop-mosquito-bites/slide/9

33 https://www.Geocaching.com/about/guidelines.aspx

34 www.project-gc.com

35 http://www.peanutsorpretzels.com/geocaching/geocach

ing-travel/
36 http://www.geocacherscompass.com/how-to-
geocache/how-to-prepare-for-a-power-trail/
37 http://www.prevention.com/mind-body/emotional-
health/spending-time-outside-relieves-stress
38
http://www.natureandforesttherapy.org/uploads/8/1/4/
4/8144400/_naturetherapyandpreventivemedicine.pdf
39 http://www.prevention.com/mind-body/emotional-
health/spending-time-outside-relieves-stress
40
http://archive.unews.utah.edu/news_releases/nature-
nurtures-creativity-2/
41 https://www.ncbi.nlm.nih.gov/pubmed/11851541
42
https://www.ahrq.gov/downloads/pub/evidence/pdf/alz
heimers/alzcog.pdf
43 https://www.verywell.com/what-you-need-to-know-
about-eustress-3145109
44 http://www.ucd.ie/news/2012/06JUN12/130612-
Socialising-helps-to-alleviate-symptoms-of-
depression.html
45 https://www.rethink.org/news-views/2016/9/marks-
blog-1
46
https://thegeocachingjunkie.com/2016/09/26/geocachi
ng-is-good-for-you-8-reasons-why/
47 http://www.webmd.com/heart-
disease/news/20131220/walk-more-to-cut-heart-
attack-and-stroke-risk-study-suggests
48 http://www.marksdailyapple.com/exercise-
protection-mild-cognitive-impairment/
49 http://www.marksdailyapple.com/the definitive-
guide-to-walking/#axzz2pegvyLob
50 http://well.blogs.nytimes.com/2015/07/22/how-
nature-changes-the-brain/?_r=0
51
http://www.npr.org/templates/story/story.php?storyId
=123108679

52 http://www.skillsyouneed.com/ips/problem-solving3.html

53 https://www.Geocaching.com/geocache/GCJ11E_chouteau-lock-17?guid=a217cb11-e67b-4bae-8fd4-42c145611252

54 https://www.geocaching.com/blog/2010/11/geocaching-com-souvenirs/

55 http://www.retrojunk.com/content/child/quote/page/4415/the-magic-school-bus

56 http://ftfgeocacher.com/

57 https://www.amazon.com/Russell-Atkinson/e/B005XMCPN0/ref=sr_ntt_srch_lnk_1?qid=1481695447&sr=1-1-catcorr

58 http://idealistcareers.org/12-quotes-that-will-encourage-you-to-follow-your-passion/

59 https://www.Geocaching.com/blog/category/geocache-of-the-week/

60 https://www.Geocaching.com/geocache/GC5F23V_here-comes-the-sun?guid=fcb45632-f766-43cc-a7d1-6f64278c3ac6

61 https://www.Geocaching.com/about/glossary.aspx

Made in the
USA
Monee, IL